SAGE was founded in 1965 by Sara Miller McCune to support the dissemination of usable knowledge by publishing innovative and high-quality research and teaching content. Today, we publish over 900 journals, including those of more than 400 learned societies, more than 800 new books per year, and a growing range of library products including archives, data, case studies, reports, and video. SAGE remains majority-owned by our founder, and after Sara's lifetime will become owned by a charitable trust that secures our continued independence.

Los Angeles | London | New Delhi | Singapore | Washington DC | Melbourne

ADVANCE PRAISE

'A timely book that brings out empathy and compassion and tells us why we need to support each other in an increasingly selfish world. In Mother Teresa's words: "If we have no peace, it is because we have forgotten that we belong to each other"'.

Jacqueline Fritschi-Cornaz, *Actress (she plays Mother Teresa in an upcoming film)*

'"The most precious gift we can offer anyone is our attention. When mindfulness embraces those we love, they will bloom like flowers," noted Thich Nhat Hanh. This has always been true but maybe even more so in this era of growing inequities and ever-increasing demands placed on our time, attention and money from all corners. Philanthropy is the ability to look beyond oneself and plant the proverbial seed for a tree whose shade you will not necessarily enjoy. It takes vision, resources and a big heart. This book traces, in a highly readable and instructive way, the evolution of altruism and philanthropy across time and across cultures. It is well researched and makes good use of real-life examples and scholarly research from various disciplines and brings to light many salient issues of the day'.

Professor Sunder Ramaswamy,
Vice Chancellor, KREA University

'This beautiful book reminds us that beyond the paradigm of philanthropy as a duty, and beyond the realm of impact investing with an eye on some return, there is a transformative quality in giving just for the joy of giving'.

Arun Maira, *Former Chairman of Boston Consulting Group, India, and Former Member of Planning Commission of India*

'This mother–daughter team makes an eloquent appeal, backed by research, for empathy and altruism, with a genuine concern for the well-being of others, which is vital for our times'.

Jairam Ramesh, *Economist and Politician*

'Philanthropy has always been a part of the Indian society, though the way we give differs from other parts of the world. This deeply insightful book explores the motivations for why people give'.

Raghav Bahl, *Serial Entrepreneur and Founder of Several Television Channels*

'Many strive to change the world, but there is nothing so heart-warming and rewarding like seeing first-hand how one has changed a single life for the better'.

Curtis S. Chin, *Former US Ambassador to the Asian Development Bank*

'I see this book coming to the world at a very interesting time; it focuses on hope and optimism rather than worrying about the world. It focuses on how the world will, could and has always come together to serve its own people.

Written from the heart, and with such tremendous love and care, it is a very interesting account of our shared responsibilities and inspires (and provokes the selfish genes!) to look beyond thy selves and beyond our boxes called "my own self".

I have had an opportunity to work with many philanthropists around the world who have either contributed their wealth or lent their voices, their time or their expertise. This book reminds us of a common denominator across those pledges, and that is the heart.

I am also touched by the fact that the book is authored by a mother–daughter duo. A relationship that transcends any other and a relationship that comes across as the force behind this beautiful narrative'.

Dr Purvi Mehta, *Head of Asia Agriculture, Bill & Melinda Gates Foundation*

'This is a truly remarkable book full of humanity and common decency. The authors understand the joy of giving and the impact of philanthropy, and now explore what altruism means and what makes people give. How and why does the act of giving transform lives, for those who give and those who receive? The stories they tell are full of humanity and conscious to the fact that people's needs include dignity. While the book is written about the basis for altruism and giving in India, it has global relevance. In a world in which there is deepening inequality and where populism is stoking fear of the other rather than compassion for our fellow human beings, I hope that it will be widely read. It deserves to be, and I trust that all who read the book will come away fuelled by the prevailing optimism that the young of today are the change-makers, more giving and forgiving than my own generation'.

Janet Anne Royall, *Baroness Royall of Blaisdon, Principal of Somerville College, University of Oxford, and Former Leader of the House of Lords*

Why People GIVE

Why People GIVE

Interpreting Altruism

Ratna and Suhasini Vira

Los Angeles | London | New Delhi
Singapore | Washington DC | Melbourne

Copyright © Ratna Vira and Suhasini Vira, 2019

All rights reserved. No part of this book may be reproduced or utilized in any form or by any means, electronic or mechanical, including photocopying, recording or by any information storage or retrieval system, without permission in writing from the publisher.

First published in 2019 by

SAGE Publications India Pvt Ltd
B1/I-1 Mohan Cooperative Industrial Area
Mathura Road, New Delhi 110 044, India
www.sagepub.in

SAGE Publications Inc
2455 Teller Road
Thousand Oaks, California 91320, USA

SAGE Publications Ltd
1 Oliver's Yard, 55 City Road
London EC1Y 1SP, United Kingdom

SAGE Publications Asia-Pacific Pte Ltd
18 Cross Street #10-10/11/12
China Square Central
Singapore 048423

Published by Vivek Mehra for SAGE Publications India Pvt Ltd. Typeset in 10.5/13pt Bembo and 11.5/13 pts in Gill Sans by Fidus Design Pvt Ltd, Chandigarh.

Library of Congress Cataloging-in-Publication Data Available

ISBN: 978-93-532-8581-4 (PB)

SAGE Team: Manisha Mathews, Namarita Kathait, Ankit Verma and Rajinder Kaur
Artwork by Ratna Vira

In the loving memory of nani

For Shauryya and Shashank
... who give wings to words

For Prema and Jyoti
... who continue to inspire

Thank you for choosing a SAGE product!
If you have any comment, observation or feedback,
I would like to personally hear from you.

Please write to me at **contactceo@sagepub.in**

Vivek Mehra, Managing Director and CEO, SAGE India.

Bulk Sales

SAGE India offers special discounts
for purchase of books in bulk.
We also make available special imprints
and excerpts from our books on demand.

For orders and enquiries, write to us at

Marketing Department
SAGE Publications India Pvt Ltd
B1/I-1, Mohan Cooperative Industrial Area
Mathura Road, Post Bag 7
New Delhi 110044, India

E-mail us at **marketing@sagepub.in**

Subscribe to our mailing list
Write to **marketing@sagepub.in**

This book is also available as an e-book.

CONTENTS

Preface ix
Acknowledgements xv

Beginnings... 1

Chapter 1
Have a Heart... 17
Live from the Heart... 24

Chapter 2
Altruism Transcends the Selfish Genes 29
A Second Chance at Life 39

Chapter 3
Origins of Altruism Meme 43
A Living Miracle 53

Chapter 4
The Game Theory of Giving... 57
The Daughter with Golden Smile 68

Chapter 5
Generosity Isn't Altruism 71
This Too Shall Pass 77

Chapter 6
What Motivates Donors? 81
Divine Intervention 87

Chapter 7
The Ultimate Aim of Altruism 91
When Prayers Are Answered 98

Chapter 8
    Transforming Lives Can Lead to Happiness 101
    A Shot at Normal Life 113

Chapter 9
    Love Is a Two-way Street 117
    Rain in the Time of Drought 125

Chapter 10
    Giving Gratitude 129
    The Heart That Pumped Dreams 137

Chapter 11
    Optimism as Art of Living 141
    Power of Hope amidst No Option 147

Chapter 12
    Grit, Focus and Determination 151
    The Hour of Happiness 155

Chapter 13
    Developing the Drive to Do Good 159
    The Spirit of Never Giving Up 163

Chapter 14
    Creating 'Impact' Through Giving 167
    Against All Odds 172
    Every Soul Is a Phoenix 176
    Light at the End of a Dark Tunnel 179
    Wishing Upon a Shooting Star 181
    A Hopeful Sky of New Beginnings 184

Chapter 15
    The Change Makers 193

Reflections 207

Bibliography 215
About the Authors 219

PREFACE

Over the past few years, I have learnt to be an observer, to watch and see what people do, to understand what their motivations are. I watch the world spin, and I feel breathless; everyone is in a hurry. Money is a number, and people are just social media profiles. I feel intimidated by the explosion of information but do not voice my doubts, convinced as I am that other people may feel differently. And, as I grow older, I find that I am pulled more and more to the past.

But, then, no one else knew my nana–nani the way I did. Grandchildren have a unique perspective; they see the past from where their story begins. They know no past and don't, as little children, care about what happens next. The future is just a word. They believe what they are told and judge only later when they piece the past together and get a perspective.

I was no different. I spent many years with my maternal grandparents, Mr H. D. Shourie and Mrs Dayawanti Shourie. My nana, who started Common Cause, worked at one end of the dining table, while I sat at the other side, doing the school homework.

Little did I realize then that he was setting up an organization that would help many many people. For nana, it was the larger picture that mattered. It was helping the masses that motivated him to draft petition after petition and present these to the courts. He would, at an advanced age, drive across to the Delhi High Court and argue the cases himself.

Nani, on the other hand, was interested in the immediate; her influence was beatific. She held people together. Her concern for those around her was genuine. From her, I learnt empathy. I learnt that every life mattered, that every person was someone. That people can get taken in and fooled in some cases, but you cannot fake empathy. Empathy is like a switch in our brains; some have it turned on and others don't. Often, people from the same family differ.

Nani was interested in everyone; she wanted to know their stories. She kept count of their problems, their growing families, shrinking budgets and so on. This she did for all. She even remembered details of her many nephews and nieces, as well as the people whom she interacted with, reaching out to help in whatever way she could. However, often this kindness would be one sided, as is seen in life. Even though they were aware of the close bonds with her and she was good to them in her lifetime, the same nieces and nephews might not be good to people she loved dearly. Life is like that. Nani was undeterred; she overlooked the slights but never gave up on people.

I was always amazed at how people shared their deepest concerns with her. At shops, after making her purchases, she would always ask almost everyone for an update, filling in little details if they left them out.

Her memory was what I marvelled at when I was younger. Today, I marvel at her empathy. Figuring out how many people she helped is, for me, like trying to guess the size of the universe. She helped in whatever way she could: she listened, she gave of herself and helped financially; but most importantly, she was there for people.

Days can stretch and feel long, but I am convinced years are short. It was Christmas; another year had flown by. I was at the hairdresser when a chance meeting with my friend, Prema, started a conversation, and ended with her whipping out her mobile and showing me photographs of children in the foundation she was running. She told me stories about them. I sat mesmerized, because the joy on the faces of those children concealed their very real problems.

There was a boy who had, until recently, been on a ventilator, battling for life, but was grinning broadly. Another, who knew she was going to be operated upon in the coming week, was enjoying the moment in the photograph. I heard about a mother who had lost her first-born but was determined to reach out and help as many little children as she could.

My chain of thoughts was broken by someone complaining about overeating; another voice joined in about the lack of party options.

I instinctively knew that the children in Prema's phone had the secret to happiness. They knew that life is like candyfloss and cannot be touched except very gently, that happiness cannot be bought and that it must be brought out in people. Life is as much about giving as it is about receiving. And happiness is not a place on earth. It is a place in the head (and since neither Elon Musk nor Richard Branson has flown to Mars yet, we can't comment on whether Mars is a happy place!).

I remember reading, 'You can only see the fall of water. You don't see how the ocean becomes the cloud'.

I realized how every good deed harnesses the secret of the ocean, and what we see is the obvious, that is, the cloud becoming the ocean as it rains. What we miss is that in giving there is a big element of getting back. And here I am not talking about karma.

Christmas spilled over to New Year, and I still could not forget those smiling faces. I mentioned them to my children, and my daughter said with the innocence of youth, 'Let's do something for them'.

'Like what?' I asked.

She shrugged and said, 'I know you; there will be something'.

Suhasini loves collecting quotes that inspire or inform. One of her favourites is, 'Do all the good you can, in all the ways you can', John Wesley, 1703–1791.

My children are my muse. My daughter came to me with a little post-it. Pointing at it, she said, 'Let's look at the economics of giving'. I have included the diagram in its original, as she drew it, on page 63. 'Did you know, game theory has a rationale for philanthropy?' she asked, and without waiting for an answer began to talk about the psychology of giving. 'There is something called Positive Altruism', she told me.

My son, Shauryya, believes I can do just about anything if I put my mind to it. He always sees a book in every situation. That was the genesis of this book (pun intended).

I met Prema again, and two conversations convinced me that I wanted to do something for her foundation and the children they were helping. However, I was floundering, toying with some ideas until Suhasini did some research and came up with the big-bucket items that went on to form the backbone of this book.

Seeing her interest, I took her with me for subsequent meetings with Prema, and, slowly, over several months, Suhasini and I began to collaborate on the book.

It has taken almost three years to research and write this book. I have taken courses on positive psychology to understand the nuances of why people give.

Suhasini and I have agreed, disagreed and fought over our turfs. Finally, as a subject expert, she has painstakingly guided the research that backs the academic writing. I had to learn from her how to make citations and record them.

She has learnt through this process—that a book is hard work, sleepless nights—and together we have kept it going even when we felt like giving up.

Suhasini has made me realize that Shauryya and her generation are the doers and the givers. Their thoughts are not barricaded by bias and preconceived notions. They are far more giving and forgiving and accepting than any generation before them were.

The process of writing this book, collaborating with a young daughter and seeing life through her eyes, has changed my worldview. Millennials, I feel, have more empathy than many of us, and interacting with them because of my writing has been an eye opener. They not only think differently but also act differently. This book cuts across generations; it is as much for readers of my age as it is for younger readers.

The quotes are some of Suhasini's favourites. The illustrations have been done by me.

This is a deeply moving book, which charts the rise of altruism across time, belief systems and cultures. This book is very relevant to the India of today, where empathy seems to be evaporating from society. *Why People Give: Interpreting Altruism* will change how we look at the act of giving and, equally importantly, how we treat each other. It draws upon the emotional courage and feisty spirit of a couple faced with personal loss who created a movement that saves the lives of many children across India. The narrative unfolds with each chapter ending with a story, that of a child who lives today because of the work done by charities and their indefatigable team of volunteers, doctors and donors. The book is passionately argued, deeply researched and filled with indelible stories of real people. It will resonate with many people, with its real-life stories, illustrations, and conversations between two fictional characters, Keira and Rita. Their conversation sums up the essence of the preceding chapter.

Suhasini brings to the book freshness of the millennial outlook, whereas I have looked at the whole idea of why sometimes it is easier for people to give to institutions rather than help a fellow human being in need.

The book is about the basis for altruism and giving in India.

We examine the act of giving from the primeval human instincts embedded in our genetic code, to exploring the psychology and economics of giving and altruism in India.

We argue, backed by research, that Indians dramatically undervalue the impulse that drives giving. The book explores what and how far are we as people willing to reach out to those whom we perceive as less fortunate than we are. The fundamental basis of caring, a cautionary account about the battle between greed and giving, and our own frailty in the face of life choices are discussed. It is a truism that conflicting issues are seldom about what is on the surface; conflicts are often about matters that remain unsaid, untreated and unhealed—about emotional wounds. We argue that individual choices about giving and altruism are also driven by a similar impulse, and that we cannot understand philanthropy without analysing the motivation for giving. Giving and caring are linked to happiness and positive psychology, and this book shows this link through extensive research.

I am the author of *Daughter by Court Order* and *It's Not About You*, and until now have been known for holding up a mirror to society in my novels. This is my first non-fiction work, which my daughter, Suhasini, and I have co-authored. Together, we hold out a brief for altruism—and why our society needs it today more than ever before. Through this book, I believe that I am reaching back in time to move forward. Looking back at trends and examining the past have thrown up reasons to believe that giving not only helps the receiver, but also the giver is helped by the afterglow of giving. In becoming better versions of ourselves, we change the world we live in. Suhasini hopes that the book will appeal to millennials and makes a passionate appeal to them for reaching out beyond their immediate environment.

Why People Give is relevant and universal in its appeal. The fault lines of inequality and divisive forces are tearing us apart. This book dares us to be better people—and, in doing so, appeals to us to be the change, to spread positivity and to make the world a better place. All it takes is a desire to help and an iron will to see it through.

My nani used to tell me that people will pull you down, will discourage you and will hold you back. And that this should not be taken personally because more often than not, you are unleashing their demons.

'Choose well: your choice is brief and yet endless'. (Ella Winter)

ACKNOWLEDGEMENTS

This book has been an interesting journey for Suhasini and me. We have learnt to collaborate, agree, disagree and then arrive at an informed decision. We have decided that all the proceeds and receipts from this book will go towards supporting the wonderful work of the Genesis Foundation.

More importantly, the study of positive psychology has helped me understand that optimism is a choice especially in the face of adversity. Writing the stories that have been included at the end of each chapter was humbling. The courage and the hope that these parents had could move mountains.

Our publisher, SAGE, was exceptional, especially Arti David and the team at SAGE, for believing in our book. We are indebted to Manisha Mathews, Namarita Kathait and Ankit Verma for their incisive remarks and edits, which have made this book tighter. Manisha nudged me into making the illustrations, and her enthusiasm at different stages of the book has kept us going.

Many friends have supported us. I would like to mention Romonika Dey Sharan, Rajiv Batra, Vickram Bahl, Dr Gursharan Lamba, Ashwajit and Tanya Singh, Deepa Tandon, Hema and Vivek Gandhi, Sushma Narain, Suhasini Haidar, Madhav Saraswat and Payal Singh; Rajika Narain for always encouraging my writing even when I falter at times; Dr Upasna Singh for being the best dentist in the world (I needed surgery and should know!) and a great friend; Aditya and Menaka Lakhanpal for their generosity and support and the millions of times I have turned to them; Kate and Tushar, thank you for your support; Uday Walia and Niti Dixit, as always indebted to both of you; Sunita Katoch, Chandigarh, for going out of her way always; Preeti Newani and

Latika (MAAC Gurgaon) for adopting me and teaching me Photoshop and other software.

A big thank you to the Aara Foundation, especially Priyal Guliani and Anami. They have dedicated their lives to raising funds to support children suffering from congenital heart defect (CHD). We are indebted to Anoop Seth and G. K. Swamy for showing how big things start from the dining table. Radhika Bharat Ram, thank you for reinforcing our belief that the giver receives much more than the recipient. You ticked every box in my positive psychology checklist. Madhav Lavakare, Jyoti Pande Lavakare and Ajay Lavakare, thank you for sharing Madhav's incredible journey.

Prema and Jyoti Sagar, it has been wonderful to discuss the manuscript at various stages while we were writing; your support has meant a lot. Simran Sagar, thank you for providing us with information that was required from time to time. Nupur and the team at the Genesis Foundation, thank you for your enthusiasm in the project and belief in it. It's wonderful to also be associated with Jacqueline Fritschi-Cornaz, who plays Mother Teresa in the upcoming film *Kavita and Teresa*. Many thanks Jacqueline for supporting our book.

Many of the stories deal with high-quality medical care and the commitment of very senior surgeons which saved many valuable children. We salute you.

I believe that Arti Mathur Lall and Anita Srivastav bring me luck along with encouragement. I thank my friend Helen Pennant for suggesting very useful books to add to our reading list and Emma Derham for encouraging us to write to the finish.

We are both indebted to Shashank for cross referencing the manuscript with physics and to Shauryya for keeping Suhasini and me going when our spirits flagged, when the research seemed endless and the book seemed like never ending.

Ruzbeh and BABA, thank you for making this possible.

—**Ratna**

Mama, thank you for believing in me and my work. You've taught me so much about writing; but more importantly, about courage, resilience and compassion.

A single sentence can't capture the depth of my affection and gratitude, but thank you Papa and Shauryya for being there for us at every step of the way and for supporting us no matter what.

Soham, for entering our lives with that one message back in class 8 and making every day brighter since then. Rushika, for redefining what friendship means to me.

Trisha, Dhruv, Ria, Abeer, Jatin, Harsh, Yashas, Tanvi and Varun, for being there for me throughout school and beyond. Aishwarya, Devika and Sayuj—childhood friends are never forgotten.

I would like to thank my teachers at Sanskriti School, New Delhi—Abha Sehgal ma'am, Kavita Soota ma'am, Sreelekha ma'am, Meenu ma'am, Manisha ma'am, Chayan ma'am, Abha Malik ma'am and Sakshi ma'am.

Dhamija Sir—you have always believed in me. Your support means a lot to me.

Duncan, Amy and Olly for being the best housemates I could've asked for. Kate, Fiona, Hannah, Apostolos, Niamh, Nanki, Kimaya and Ellen—university wouldn't have been half as amazing (or even survivable!) without all of you in it.

—**Suhasini**

BEGINNINGS

Be happy, and a reason will come along.
—Robert Brault

I saw a child who was living but dead.

Ravi[1] stared at the wall mutely, gazing outwards but not looking at anything in particular. His eyes were indeed open, but they were blank, soulless. Yet even his vacant gaze held meaning, and his eyes were the door to his world. If anyone spoke to him, he would close his eyes to shut out the world, to block the noise.

He lay there, staring at the wall all day and late into the night. There was no today, no tomorrow for him. Time held no meaning and had no boundaries, night and day had merged.

Ravi intrigued me. His solitary existence to me was not lonely. I empathized with him. I saw in him a kindred soul. The busy world judged him by the way he looked. And I of all people knew what that meant and how deeply it hurt.

He had not shut out the world without reason. He had retreated to a place of safety. The darkness was comforting.

---

[1] Names have been changed to protect the identity of the individuals.

The blank peeling wall would not hurt him, abandon him. It was there when he fell asleep, when he woke up and for the long hours in between. He felt safe knowing that some things would not change. He clung to his little spot in the world, his wall.

The world, uncaring about the Ravis of the world, passed him by, giving up on him. As he retreated into himself, people gave up on him and forgot him.

And I never knew him until one day, by chance, his world and mine touched each other.

I watched him. Upon seeking to help, I was advised to look at other children because he was a 'gone-case'. Even those who cared for him had given up and my time would perhaps be better spent elsewhere. But I identified with that gone-case and his hopelessness got me going.

Being contrary and stubborn is sometimes a blessing. The trouble this streak has got me into! And I just don't take No for an answer!

And so time passed, and I began my lonely drives with Ravi at the back of my blue Maruti van. The first drive and many more that were to follow.

Ravi initially blocked me out. He would shut his eyes as he was carried to my car, tensing his body, and holding his breath until his face turned red. We would drive in silence.

And then … one day … I heard something. Not quite sure, I stopped the car, got off and walked to the back of the car where he lay cushioned in pillows so that he would not roll and hurt himself. It was a cold winter morning; the roads of Delhi were deserted. I looked up at the sky. The breaking yellow sun looking like a child's happy drawing, with all its rays streaming outwards and a big smile on its face.

He looked me straight in the eyes, did Ravi, and continued with what I later realized was his singing. I stared at him. His face framed by a blue hoodie was a shade of pink that was just turning red; his chapped lips grinned at me cheekily as we shared a moment.

And I got back into the driving seat. And then there was no looking back.

A few questions and a little prodding helped me understand his situation better.

Ravi was born to a roadside vendor. A slow learner from birth, his problems grew with age. He dragged his left leg, as his left side was affected by cerebral palsy. Cerebral palsy is a lifelong condition affecting movement and coordination. It was probably due to some problem with his brain before, during or soon after birth.

The children in his village teased him, imitating his limp. The elders in the village taunted his father by referring to him as the cripple's father. Ravi was too slow and far too weak to help his father with work; he was the son his father had no use for. He was a burden.

His mother tried to shield him, hiding him when his father came home at night. But she could not prevent what happened one night. Ravi's father came home in a drunken rage, picked up his son and flung him into the village well.

The cries were heard by villagers who pulled him out several hours later. The well had probably run dry in the summer. Ravi had spent hours alone, terrified at the bottom of the well…broken. No wonder that he distrusted people!

The feudal patriarchal system is strong in parts of India, and the villagers did not want to tangle with Ravi's father. The best course of action, they reasoned, was that they help the mother send the boy to someone who might care for him. The caring and concern did not go beyond bringing Ravi to a hospital in Old Delhi. They had neither the money nor the understanding to do more than that. They handed him over to the hospital and, the next day, the mother and the villagers left. The rest was in the hands of destiny and their conscience was clear.

The hospital contacted the Missionaries of Charity and that is how Ravi found in their blank walls his best friend.

I would often walk across and talk to him. He would never answer back, going into his shut-your-eyes-and-this-irritating-person-will-go-away routine. I would be sweetly told that his chances of survival were, at best, abysmally low. A friendly volunteer once guided me away, saying that I should not set myself up for heartbreak. But I was drawn to Ravi, and my feet would find themselves next to his bed.

Karma comes in many forms. My husband's client, an American, was in town and he had done the sightseeing, visiting the Red Fort and the Qutab Minar on an earlier trip. He wanted to see something different, the real India.

I bundled him into my blue Maruti van and drove him to see Ravi and the other children.

We spent an intensely disappointing afternoon together. Ravi had ignored me. What had I expected? I was not quite sure, but I was acutely hurt. On the way back, Eugene Mihaly, a management consultant in the United States, just would not speak and I did not want to speak either.

I decided, then, that I would change the situation and went back the next day. I started to look for hospitals and physiotherapy clinics where I could take Ravi. Finally, the long painful physiotherapy sessions began. Every Thursday afternoon, I would bundle him into my blue van and take him for his sessions. The pain would be unbearable, leaving Ravi writhing and howling. This was the early days of physiotherapy after all. It would be too much, and I would ask them to stop.

It was during one of the trips to the hospital, at the South Extension red light, that I heard the soft humming. It was a cold winter morning, but it felt warm as though the breaking sun was smiling down at me.

It was amazing, the moment I heard Ravi singing to himself in the back. He was happy! It was a breakthrough, and I was exhilarated.

But my joy was short-lived. The doctors told me not to waste my money on him and take up the cause of another child who needs it more. 'This one will not live out the year', they said.

When did you become God? I remember asking the doctor as I wheeled Ravi out to the car and settled him in. The boy had lowered his eyelids and shut his eyes tight. He had heard the doctor, understood what was being discussed and feared that I too would give up on him. For the hospital and the doctors, he was a gone-case; he no longer existed; his future had been erased. His joyrides too would come to an end. There was nothing to look forward to.

I was angry. He was sad. We drove back in silence. But I did not give up.

My journey to the soul began from here. In helping him, I connected with myself.

Well-meaning offers of help came. A French lady in India volunteered to follow up with other doctors. She had the right intent but set Ravi back several steps. The medical file was lost and with it his medical history.

It was not easy without medical papers, but we drew upon old friendships to access the All-India Institute of Medical

Science or AIIMS, as it is popularly known. We took one Sunday at a time, driving Ravi across Delhi to AIIMS. And we squeezed out our happiness, Ravi singing at the back as I drove humming along.

Waiting at AIIMS one day, I watched an old man pace the corridor. His distress was clear. Finally, when I could not take it anymore, I went up and talked to him.

His child was very unwell, needed surgery, but he did not have the money for it. I promised to help, telling him that I would be back the next day. These were early days in our careers, so my husband and I did not have the resources ourselves. But we had enough friends willing to help, and they did.

I went back but the bed was empty, and he was sitting slumped next to it, clutching unpaid bills.

His tears told me the story, no words were needed. I felt helpless, I felt his despair.

I felt my own loss acutely, but it was not that or seeing Ravi that moved me to do some of the work I do. It was this one incident at AIIMS that was the catalyst for change.

As the father paced the corridor, counting and re-counting the money he held in his hands, I identified with him, because I was doing the same for Ravi.

I cannot forget my conversation with him. 'I will sell my land, I will sell everything but will not give up on my son madamji', he had told me. I had watched them and had promised to help them the next day, but the next day had been too late.

They had been forgotten by the third day, and no one could tell me where to find them. Not surprising for a hospital where patients from across the country jostle for space and attention, sharing beds and even floor space, just so they could get the treatment they need.

I never found the old man and his wife, but their life moved me and gave me a purpose beyond myself. I had lost my child, a little heart, but hoped to save as many children as I could—one day at a time, one child at a time.

It began as our personal quest, my husband and mine. His support buoyed me on.

We would often go to the Missionaries of Charity, valuing the selfless work they did for those who had no one to support them. One day, a child clambered on to my husband's lap and held on to him and just sobbed. The child held on to him for hours, finding comfort in his arms. We were moved by the child's need, the human connect; it is fragile and yet strong.

A sleepless night for us! We wanted to adopt the child, and almost did. The reality of life came in the way. Bringing him home meant that we would not be able to help other children. We had two children and they were already a handful. Careers and children meant we were stretched as young professionals. Adopting a child and bringing up the three would have filled our home but drained our resources, preventing us from reaching out to other children. A tough choice, but we did not go back to the children's home. The baby found loving parents and moved on, leaving us wistfully happy.

For us it was a turning point. We made a conscious decision not to get emotionally invested in the children we cared for. Easier said than done, but we trained ourselves over time.

That night, we decided that we wanted to help children with critical illnesses. We wanted to give them a chance to live. This was decades ago, when medicine was not as advanced as it is today. Yet, early intervention meant a 98 per cent success rate.

We were still struggling with Ravi and how to get him medical help when we heard from Eugene. He had mobilized medical help in the United States and asked us to send him there!

We were exhilarated, the nuns at the Missionaries of Charity were thrilled, but it was still an uphill task to deal with all the bureaucracy. The biggest problem was the US visa. The visa counsellor rejected the application, saying that Ravi would never come back and that he was a flight risk.

Time, however, was on our side. India's economy was opening up. I persisted with the embassy and said, 'If you do not give him a visa, I will have Mother Teresa standing here tomorrow!' Sure enough, we had the visa. We had to get an airline to carry him lying down. My dear friend Kavin Sethi, who was at Lufthansa, helped. An entire row was taken out to fit him, and the staff was just remarkable.

The nuns were sorry to see him go. We broke our rule; Ravi meant so much to us. He spent a couple of days at home with us before boarding the flight. Detachment was an alien word that night as we said our byes.

We heard from him often. His health improved, but he was still not able to function without help.

And then, one day, we heard that he was being adopted by a Christian couple who had lost their son in a road accident. Had he survived, he would have been in a wheelchair and so, in Ravi, they found their child.

His photographs showed him well adjusted in his new home. Slowly his calls became less frequent. Life moved on.

THE HEART REVEALS ITSELF

Sheela[2] was a young girl growing up in a small village in Madhya Pradesh, India. All was good in her little world. Like many other girls, her life was routine until she hit puberty.

Overnight, one day, parts of her face began to disappear. Huge boils appeared, and as they receded, parts of her face just vanished. Her chin and cheekbones stuck out oddly because the flesh that held them together had disappeared.

The villagers shunned her, and then they began to avoid her family. They proclaimed her a witch.

And one night her parents turned her out of the home.

While passing a field, a priest heard the sound of a young child crying. On looking around, he found a girl with tears flowing down an exposed cheekbone. A frightening sight! The priest brought her to Delhi and took her to doctors. The doctors had seen a lot, but Sheela was a challenge even for them. Scared, lonely and with a face that seemed to be disintegrating fast, she was in a difficult mess. Her face was misshapen, and the wounds were exposed.

The doctors started working on her face; but due to very little support, they finally stopped the treatment. The priest reached out to Mother Teresa's Missionaries of Charity home in Old Delhi.

Her eyes spoke to me. Her despair, her abject hopelessness moved me. I went from pillar to post trying to get her condition diagnosed and then start the treatment.

During those days we forged a bond; Sheela slowly opened up to speak.

---

[2] Names have been changed to protect the identity of the individuals.

She talked to me, would phone me. This was before mobile phones had become ubiquitous. I would answer a call on the landline and find Sheela on the other end.

You find friends in different situations and just as I helped Sheela, she too helped me get over my loss.

Eugene was there for us and brought in a renowned plastic surgeon in America transforming lives through the art of plastic and reconstructive surgery. He had done remarkable work for cleft-chin children in Latin America.

The surgeon saw her reports and fortunately agreed to take her case. Sheela would need a lot of work, 17 surgeries for facial reconstruction. She hardly had a nose, just holes for nostrils. These would be complicated, exhausting surgeries.

Visas were easier for a funded medical case, but when I made a few calls, I was told that airlines would not carry her, given the distressing condition of her face. Stubborn as ever, I phoned airline after airline. Even now, the responses I got from some of those airlines disgust me. Finally, a friend in Air India helped with flights to the United States.

Once there, a Vietnamese American family looked after Sheela. Initially they volunteered to take care of her temporarily, but then they decided to adopt her.

A very warm and wonderful family—they have 13 children, out of which only one is their biological child. And no one knows which one. Each of the children has flourished under their care. They graduated from Berkeley, Stanford, and other top universities.

Sheela had a difficult time adjusting to the United States initially, and she would call often. And then her voice changed, she got an American accent and a new life.

In-between surgeries, she was off cycling and enrolled in a school.

Her calls became fewer and we held back too, happy in her happiness.

Years flew by and then we received an invitation for her wedding. She married a white American man, an accomplished gentleman with a heart of gold.

Sheela has two grown-up sons and her hands are full with caring for her family. She is in touch with Ravi and never fails to call me on Christmas.

Happiness is not merely a function of who we are. In her book *This Is Just My Face, Try Not to Stare*, Hollywood actress Gabourey Sidibe talks about being judged for the way she looks, about how no one sees beyond her body, and therefore misses out on seeing her as she sees herself—as a human being with feelings (Sidibe 2017).

And every human being deserves a chance.

LOOKING BEYOND THE FACE

Slicing into the crisp mountain air with the confidence of a Master, two hands spear alternately in rapid, martial movements. They belong to 15-year-old Rama. She has a karate tournament at school, and her eye is set on the black belt. This is a story of determination and self-belief. The parents and philanthropists came together to script a new life for a very sick child.

A short bout of coughing interrupts her practice. The familiar dread creeps up her spine as a reflex, but she remembers the kind words of the doctor, and mutters to herself, 'I am well, and nothing can stop ME'. Gathering courage, she tells herself, 'This is a mild viral infection; my heart is now fully fit and beating fine. And I can beat this viral'.

But this wasn't always so. A cough in the past was a sign of things going downhill rapidly. It was a warning signal. Rama's life had been a warp and weft of hospitals, medicines, surgeries and pain.

Born in May 2003, Rama was the second child of Radha and Ravish, a simple couple living in Palakkad in Kerala. They were content with their life. Ravish was an auto-rickshaw driver and earned enough to look after the family, although they never had money for luxuries.

It was a normal delivery, and Radha was relieved that it had all gone well. Their son was, unlike most brothers, not disappointed that the baby was a girl. He was excited that he now had a little sister to play with and look after.

Two weeks after birth, the celebrations came crashing down. The happiness was short-lived, because the parents could not ignore her abnormal and raspy breathing. They rushed her to a government hospital, the same one where she was born.

The doctors overlooked the family's concerns and pinned it down as a normal occurrence sometimes for babies that young. They were told that if these symptoms persisted, they could return after a month.

In the meantime, Rama developed high fever and returned to the hospital almost immediately. This time, the doctors could not dismiss the parent's fears and gave the family the reference of a private nursing home where an echocardiogram was conducted on the tiny baby girl.

The test results morphed into a nightmare; their baby girl was suffering from a life-threatening heart disorder. She had a hole in the heart, and because of the complications that were present there was no guarantee that the girl could survive.

It was as if the ground beneath them gave way; they were numbed, paralysed with fear—holding on tight to the little child in their arms. The parents found it hard to understand the medical jargon; what got through to them was that their daughter was unwell and needed immediate attention if she were to live. Their understanding of heart disorder and the steps that should be taken in this instance were limited.

To add to their woes was the lack of funds juxtaposed with the doctors urging them to admit their child, stressing that time could not be wasted.

Their resources and finances were constrained. They returned home, dazed, confused and at a complete loss on how to get Rama the medical help she urgently required. Their life suddenly seemed inadequate as money became a big issue.

Time passed; the family did not act on getting any surgery done nor did they take any more medical advice. They felt inadequate and decided to brave it since surgery without money was not an option, and they had another child to look after.

Rama's health was a recurring problem; the coughs and colds persisted. At the age of four, her parents put her into school, and that made matters worse.

Participating in sports was impossible; she could not run like other children and always lagged. Rama coped as best as she could; she just excused herself from sports and focused on studying instead.

A couple of years later, when she was in the fifth grade, she fainted at school and turned blue. Radha and Ravish rushed to school and found their daughter lying in a heap on the cold school floor. They bundled her into their arms, and a nervous Ravish brought her home in his auto-rickshaw.

Rama finally regained consciousness in the familiar surroundings of her own home. This was the turning point, and her parents decided to get medical help even if it meant venturing into the scary world beyond their village.

They took her to a hospital in Coimbatore, Tamil Nadu, where they were confronted with bad news yet again. The doctors were blunt. Their daughter needed surgery; without it her life would not extend beyond a couple of years at the outside.

Emotionally distraught, they returned home and decided once again to resume their day-to-day activities and keep Rama in school for as long as she could cope, bracing themselves for the worst.

In 2014, Rama's uncle decided to take the family to Miot Hospital, where once again an echocardiogram was conducted. The ramifications of the disease were explained to the parents, and their options were discussed. They admitted Rama into the hospital, where an angiography was conducted. The test results all pointed to the same—surgery was her only option and the success rate was between 80 and 85 per cent. These were odds that Radha and Ravish could live with. They were given a window of six months to put the money together for the operation.

Finally, they had an answer, a solution to alleviate her suffering. They were focussing on the positive and deliberately ignored what could go wrong.

The question that bothered them most and filled their days with despair was the maths, the figures and finance issues. How were they to afford this surgery?

They had two young children, and the daily expenses were exploding, which had added stress to their already difficult lives. The six months came and went, but Radha and Ravish didn't find the money for Rama.

In August 2015, Rama had to be rushed to Miot again. This time the situation was much worse. She was in bad shape, and immediate surgery was the only option.

Radha and Ravish had to make a decision. Between the two of them, Ravi as an auto-rickshaw driver and Radha as an *Aanganwadi* (early-childhood care home) worker, they earned ₹10,000 a month. They had their son to think about as well. How were they supposed to arrange ₹300,000 for the surgery? It was well beyond their means.

And, then, a faint light emerged at the end of the dark tunnel. The Director of Paediatric Cardiac Surgery at Miot Hospital got in touch with charitable foundations for financial support and the Genesis Foundation stepped in to help.

Rama was finally operated on in August 2015, in a procedure called a Double Switch. After two weeks, she was discharged when she was in a stable condition. Post-surgery care had her on medication for the next six months, after which she is on a long-term follow-up routine.

Rama is now in the ninth grade at school. Besides karate, she loves to play badminton. Headstrong and determined, Rama excels in studies. Her favourite subject is English Literature.

She has posted a quote in English on the front door of her house and it reads: 'Jump and you will find out how to unfold your wings as you fall', Ray Bradbury.

HAVE A HEART

You can't believe people when they look you in the eyes. You gotta' look behind them. See what they're standing in front of. What they're hiding.
—Sam Shepard

Have a Heart … a powerful metaphor, evoking emotional and psychological well-being, showing caring and compassion. Everyone has a heart, a physical one, but is the modern emphasis on reason, rationality and the brain pushing aside the spiritual relationship of the heart with the 'soul'? Is the heart no longer the representation of feelings for our community?

Repeated instances of altruistic behaviour, of continuing charity, are evidence that people still feel their heart as a representation of their self, of the emotional self, which cannot be reduced to materialistic, biological terms.

According to Hinduism, the heart is the connecting link between the heaven and the earth. The heart, being the obvious physical manifestation of life itself, had great significance for ancient religions. With a beating heart came life, and without it was the reality of death. Many mystic traditions regarded the heart as the hub, the centre of life.

Hinduism gave the heart a special position. It was the place of *Brahman*, the supreme cosmic spirit. Creation and all that exists have *Brahman* at its centre. And the heart is where *Brahman* resides.

The heart was also where the soul rested; it was the physical manifestation of the soul. Through the heart, the other organs were nourished and kept alive. The body procreated, it was thought, because of the heart.

While details of the brain were unknown in the early Vedic period, thoughts and emotions, and consciousness itself, came from the mind. But, as the soul rested in the heart, it was also the source of dreams and meditative thought. True consciousness, therefore, came from the heart and not from the mind. The ultimate desire was to become one with *Brahman,* and that could come about through connecting your heart to the heart of *Brahman* through duty, service, sacrifice, devotion and charity.

The Ancient Greeks, too, regarded the heart as the centre of the human body, again because the beating heart demonstrated life. It was regarded as melding the mind and body with divinity, and the heart was the seat of the soul. The heart was the driving force of the body, and our relationship with God, our character and our emotional well-being were all a consequence of having a heart.

Charity, generosity and specifically the giving of alms are regarded as virtuous in most Indian philosophies and religions. *Daana*, a Sanskrit/Pali word denoting charity and giving, came from the heart. *Daana* traces its roots to Vedic traditions and can take the form of helping individuals in need, or in the wider form of helping many through public works and philanthropy. Traditionally, *Daana* implied the relinquishment or giving up of something that was one's own to help someone without expecting anything in return. Related, but not as powerful, were the concepts of *Paropkara* (benevolent deeds), *Dakshina* (gift or fee to Guru or someone else) and *Bhiksha* (alms). *Daana* was usually given to a person or a small group, but the concept also encompassed wider charitable projects with public benefits.

Popular projects included *sarais* (rest houses), schools and care home, provision of drinking water and the planting of trees.

The Upanishads (500 BCE) contained some of the earliest discussions of *Daana*. In the Brihadaranyaka Upanishad, the three characteristics of a good, developed person are defined as self-restraint, compassion or love for all sentient life and charity (*Daana*).

Centuries later, the Bhagavad Gita gave a more practical definition of *Daana*, charity, in action. There were right and wrong forms of *Daana*. The good, enlightened charity, was given without expectation of return. But it was also to be given at the proper time and place, and to a worthy person. Egocentric charity was one given with the expectation of some return or given grudgingly. The worst form of charity was that which was given to an unworthy person or at a wrong place and time.

The Mahabharata finds repeated mention of the 'worthy person factor' in determining the value of charity. Vidur, a great scholar and the half-brother of the King Dhritarashtra, had lengthy conversations with the king about policies and governance. The Vidur Niti, the oral record passed through generations of the conversations, specifically mentions misused charity and poor utilization of wealth. Money was misused if charity were given to the unworthy or if it were denied to the worthy. A stone tied to the neck and being thrown in water was the reward offered for misused charity. Worth of the recipient and timing of the charity were as important as the mere giving of it.

Romantic poetry, in the East and the West, continued to reinforce the link of the heart to emotions and to giving. A person could be cold-hearted, tender-hearted or warm-hearted. For the romantics, the giving and the charity were ends in themselves, independent of the worthiness of the receiver.

In a more cynical and brutal world, newspaper headlines no longer stun us. Our apathy is so strong. A girl is abandoned, daughters killed, women raped and families found murdered.

These stories no longer move us. Ponzi schemes bankrupt families, farmers commit suicide. Millionaires are made, and some led to prison. 'Karma', we mutter, 'catching up'. Ingenuous ways to multiply and quadruple wealth and dodge tax are revealed daily.

All the while, the same people are seen supporting the latest causes, visiting the temples and houses of prayer, and washing their sins through giving. Is this truly charity? Is it altruism or merely selfish behaviour?

Compassion and emotion are passé. We live in the digital age surrounded by millennials who use Emojis and Instagram to express themselves, and with them most of us are forgetting life as we once knew it. We forget the heart and meticulously count 'Likes' on Facebook posts. We believe that Facebook and WhatsApp are free. What we are just beginning to realize is that in using them, we have begun to give up our freedom. In wanting to be connected all the time, our loneliness gets amplified.

The problem is that no one seems to have enough, so where is there anything to give someone else? We are all chasing the good life, and nothing seems to cut it. Greed and avarice have moved from being deadly sins to a way of life. The more you have, the more you want, and the Ferris wheel never stops.

However, money does not seem to be the glue that binds people together. In a series on the lives of the super-rich on the History Channel, it was observed that they had the same insecurities as those with very little. Their wealth became their biggest insecurity, putting their lives at risk. So, the billionaire spends his life surrounded by body guards and then hires detectives to shadow his body guards who know too much about him and his family. He sends his kids to college wanting them to experience life and so-called normalcy but is worried about who they interact with and has their friends and associates shadowed and the boyfriend investigated. Beyond a point, the wealth that is meant to give happiness morphs into something else instead of protecting the individual from the hardships of life; it often is the reason that the person needs protection.

In the words of the Nigerian poet Ben Okri, the world is a bizarre place and spinning out of control. Most people numbly watch the suffering of others glad that they are not part of the statistics. We pass the blame around, tossing it in the air, forwarding message without reading them, dressing our apathy in pithy arguments.

> Political cladding, economic cladding, intellectual cladding — things that look good but have no centre, have no heart, only moral padding. They say the words but the words are hollow They make the gestures and the gestures are shallow. (Okri 2017)

It is this view that has compelled this book to be written. The need to believe that the heart still beats, that humanity still has a chance. Counting cars and houses, clothes and parties, rocks on fingers is all good but life is meant to be measured by something far deeper, more sustainable, and although this book cannot give answers, it does attempt to show you how small changes can give hope. A trickle can become a downpour, covering the distance between words and the truth.

We need to see each other and relate to society. We need to see with our souls and reach out with our hearts. Look back and look ahead and carry people with you. Pause; help as you rush through your day. Count your blessings, and in your prayers, include someone else's troubles.

In the age of biopics in India, actor Dharmendra's words ring true. He said that he did not want a book, or a movie made on his life because people forget. And the world moves on. A strong sentiment but so true.

What does remain, however, is the echo of our actions. Do good without the sword of karma hanging over you, but because you have a heart that beats with compassion.

The real-life stories preceding the chapters are testimonies that giving can be without the hope of receiving anything back. They are also about facing adversity and getting over it. On re-engineering happiness, of recalibrating your life from the inside out. And the artist Marc Chagall once said:

> 'If I create from the heart almost everything works:
> if from the head almost nothing'.

But not everyone believes that sharing what one has is good. The ability to give does not mean the same thing as the propensity to give; this is a basic human characteristic.

'They did not die when they died; their deaths happened long before. It happened in the minds of people who never saw them. It happened in the profit margins. It happened in the laws. They died because money could be saved and made'. (Okri 2017)

India is a poor country where the disparity between the rich and the poor is stark. We are a developing nation with third-world problems, but greed and apathy drive the so-called developed nations as much as any other country. Ben Okri wrote as a reaction to the horror of the fire in Grenfell tower in London. He wrote of greed and horror, greed and apathy, greed and lack of compassion.

But, at the same time, there was the brightness of the human spirit, the sharing of hearts, and the charity of the common person.

Keira is a millennial and is in conversation with her much older colleague, Rita. She loves picking her co-worker Rita's brain on subjects that interest her, such as how much to give? Whom should one help? and so on. Rita, being much older and someone who had read up a lot on the subject, loves to discuss these questions with Keira. Throughout the book, these two grapple with questions that concern many. We bring you snippets of these conversations in each chapter. These questions may be issues that you deal with when you think about giving. Following is one of the questions posed by Keira to Rita.

Keira: 'I have good karma, I pray every day and never walk past a poor beggar without giving him something'.

Rita: 'Praying and giving are not interchangeable with karma'. And, 'Do you know that begging is a punishable crime in India? The begging industry in India is estimated to be worth over US$1.5 billion. Some are forced to beg, while many are coerced into begging; it is almost an industry. By giving alms we are contributing to the sustenance of organized crime. While it would be heartless to refuse someone who says they haven't eaten in days, it is futile to think that by giving alms you will be able to change anything. This is a deep-rooted problem and will need to be dealt with differently'.

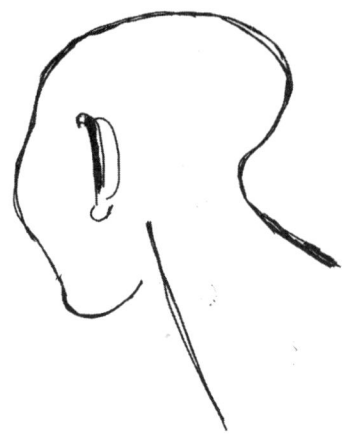

LIVE FROM THE HEART

It's your life; you don't need someone's permission to live the life you want. Be brave to live from your heart.
—Roy T. Bennett

This is a true story. Like so many of the stories in this book. A story that is full of hope and real courage in the face of great despair. It is the story of a brave mother and an innocent child. It is a story that exemplifies the unparalleled love of a grandfather for his grandchild.

It is, above all, a story that tugs at the heart, pulls at the core of our humanity and shows that love has no bank balance. It shows that love is unconditional, and that real courage has no caste no creed. Courage is not the preserve of any particular social stratum.

'For you only know how strong you are, when being strong is your only option'. Bob Marley's famous quote resonated with what Juhi and her father felt when little Uma was born. But their lives had taken a turn that would need real courage.

Bihar is one of the less developed states in India, rich in natural resources and yet backward in many ways. Social and political issues have plagued Bihar since Independence. The mind-set in society and the attitude of people are patriarchal, with the caste system still having a firm grip on the social psyche in the region.

Uma lives in Palwari Shariff, a village in Bihar, with her mother and grandfather. She was born with a CHD called Tetralogy of Fallot. She had a hole between the lower chambers of the heart and an obstruction from the heart to the lungs. There was a solution, but that needed several fairly serious surgeries. And if that wasn't heartbreaking enough, her father decided that he couldn't handle this misfortune and deserted the family soon after birth. And society … far from supporting the now single mother, Juhi, turned against her. The mother was taunted by society and shunned for having given birth to a weird sickly child and that too a daughter. 'Not worth fretting over', the village elders told her. 'Get your daughter married again', Juhi's father was repeatedly told, 'and leave that sick child, it's God's will'.

Juhi had to earn, so she started teaching young children and took tuition classes to supplement the monthly household income. She had not gone to college, so she had to teach only the youngest children with whatever she remembered from her school days. Uma and her mother, Juhi, eked out a living and managed because they were supported by Juhi's father, who continued to work hard and long hours despite his age, and only to support his daughter and sick granddaughter. He is a mechanic and manages to earn about ₹6,000 every month.

The local doctors had been reasonably accurate in their diagnosis and surgery had been advised. Juhi and her father were despondent, for they did not know what they should do. The money for the surgery was an impossible dream. They did the best they could, choosing to ignore Uma's declining health, and lived from one day to another, grateful that she had survived this long.

However, her declining health did not let them rest, and their inaction gnawed at their conscience. They approached banks for a loan. Lacking collateral, they were turned down every time. It seems that banks lend money only to those who don't need the money anyways, but the callousness of the people Juhi and her father met left them beside themselves and feeling hopeless.

Hope comes in different forms. One day, Uma's grandfather was talking to a man while fixing his car. Casual conversation turned to important concerns; one thing led to another and the story of Uma's condition and her need for immediate surgery was discussed. The man listened quietly and, like many before him had done, promised that he would try and help and would see what he could do. Uma's grandfather shook his head and carried on with his day. False, unkept promises did not impress him.

However, the man returned. He wrote down the case history, met Uma and contacted a philanthropic foundation. The rest as they say is history.

In 2015, Uma underwent her first surgery at Max Hospital, paid for by altruists and subsidized by the hospital. A successful surgery, but it still required long-term follow-up. During one of the subsequent medical checks, it was noticed that she had significant obstruction in the left pulmonary artery. Juhi and Uma clutched each other—their fear was palpable. The grandfather groaned, as he remembered Uma's discomfort and slow recovery from the first surgery. The doctors felt that an immediate surgery was needed to remove the blockage.

The family could not afford the surgery; financially, it was beyond them. They were proud and grateful and did not want to approach the Genesis Foundation again, so they went to a local moneylender who turned them down.

They decided to take Uma back to Bihar and left it to God.

The doctors at Max Hospital took it upon themselves to inform the foundation, which rose to the occasion and financially supported Uma's surgery once again. For Juhi, the foundation is her God. They saved her daughter from near death not once but twice.

Today, Uma enjoys going to school. On the rare occasion that she must be in hospital; it is the thought of school and her friends that hastens her recovery. Hope is the biggest antidote to despair and that has been the positive aspect to every single passing day in Uma's life since her operations.

Juhi is relieved that the second surgery was successful, and Uma is truly on her way to full recovery. Uma is an incredibly happy child, at ease with other children her age. Despite the hardships that she has faced as a mother, Juhi has big dreams for her daughter. 'Uma's life will be different, she will touch the stars', she tells the doctors at every follow-up appointment.

She wants her daughter to be happy and wants Uma to follow her dreams in being whatever she wants to be. Not surprisingly, at this stage, Uma wants to be a doctor! Uma aims to study hard, to gain as much knowledge as possible, and then be skilled enough to help other children like her by becoming a doctor.

Every evening as Uma plays with other children her age, Juhi gets teary, for she knows that she may not have lived had it not been for the prompt medical intervention that saved her life. Uma is the centre of Juhi's life. Her grandfather dotes on her; she is their love and their life.

'It is the existence of the foundation that has made me believe in miracles', says Juhi. She laughs loudly as she, in broken English, repeats a famous quote, 'Just when the caterpillar thought that the world is over it became a butterfly'.

'That sums up our lives and gives us hope, for there is a butterfly in each one of us', Juhi reminds me as she picks up her things, rushing for the next tuition class. Her class size has grown, and she is more confident of tackling life head on with a healthy Uma at her side.

2
ALTRUISM TRANSCENDS THE SELFISH GENES

We ought to do good to others as simply as a horse runs, or a bee makes honey, or a vine bears grapes season after season without thinking of the grapes it has borne.
—Marcus Aurelius

Let us begin our exciting journey for discovering the genesis of altruism in the 1830s on the Beagle with Charles Darwin.

Darwin's discovery of natural selection and his 1859 book *On the Origin of Species*[3] was to become the foundation of evolutionary biology, having introduced the scientific theory that populations

---

[3] More completely, '*On the Origin of Species by Means of Natural Selection, or the Preservation of Favoured Races in the Struggle for Life*', published on 24 November 1859.

evolve over the course of generations through a process of natural selection. However, it was his inference that there is a struggle for survival within and amongst species that we are most concerned about. Survival of the fittest seems to have little place for altruism and charity. Are human being exceptions to evolutionary biology?

To avoid getting drawn into theological debates or arguments about science and spirituality, we must examine the key facts and inferences of Darwin's theory of evolution. Drawing upon a similar argument to that of Thomas Malthus[4] a few decades earlier, Darwin realized that fertile populations were abundant and would grow exponentially, while the resources to support those abundant populations were limited or perhaps even scarce. To check growing populations, there could be conflict that raised the death rate, or environmental degradation that lowered the birth rate.

The evolutionary argument infers that the stable population sizes that Darwin observed, along with relatively stable food and environmental resources, could only have come about through a struggle for survival and the settling down into a state of equilibrium amongst the species. Further, the individuals less suited to the environment are less likely to survive and less likely to reproduce; individuals more suited to the environment are more likely to survive and more likely to reproduce and leave their heritable traits to future generations, which produces the process of natural selection. Darwin's 'survival of the fittest' really meant that only the stable forms of life would survive. Natural selection merely favoured stable life forms and rejected unstable ones.

---

[4] He argued that population growth generally expanded in times and in regions of plenty until the size of the population relative to the primary resources caused distress: 'Yet in all societies, even those that are most vicious, the tendency to a virtuous attachment is so strong that there is a constant effort towards an increase of population. This constant effort as constantly tends to subject the lower classes of the society to distress and to prevent any great permanent amelioration of their condition'. (Malthus 1798)

By now, evolution working by natural selection and survival of the fittest is a respected and well-acknowledged theory. But who survives? The individual, the species or something else? When we are discussing altruism, these questions truly matter. If survival were for groups as a whole, perhaps species, then the individual would not matter. The individual could be altruistic, could even be sacrificed, for the good of the group or the species. The individual would not matter, and natural selection would favour groups where people were individually willing to sacrifice themselves for the greater good. The world would, eventually, find itself filled with truly altruistic, self-sacrificing people, willing to die for the larger good of humanity.

And this is where group selection starts to break down. Within this group of self-sacrificing individuals would be a random minority of selfish people, ready to make use of the goodness of the others. This smaller group would be better equipped to survive, as they would get a disproportionate part of the assets and resources of the group. The selfish group would pass on these survival traits to their children, and the wider group would, in a few generations, have an undistinguishable mix of altruistic and selfish persons. It is hard to imagine pure altruistic groups, with no contact with others who might not be as selfless as they themselves are.

The alternative is, of course, selection at a lower level of organization than the group as a whole.

The power of Darwin's theory of evolution by natural selection, with its model of branching common descent, can be applied to a range of biological, geological and agricultural sciences. Almost at once, the theory was used as an analogy in economic and political debates, with capitalists arguing that natural selection supported the idea of low government intervention in the economy, and others opposed them to say that positive action was required to remove social and economic inequities. Most political and economic commentaries, however, had only a superficial understanding of Darwin's scientific theory. They were drawn to the analogy and came from other preconceived concepts of social progress and evolution.

Our concern is not with analogies, even though they are at best broad guides to an argument and not facts in themselves. The central question we are drawn to is whether altruistic behaviour flies in the face of our origins as living beings. Are we destined to be in a struggle for survival, where helping one another actually hurts the individual who offers the help?

Richard Dawkins, a modern evolutionary biologist, and a leader in the attempts to increase the public understanding of science, takes a more specific view on where the struggle for survival takes place. It is in our genetic code, says Dawkins in his path-breaking 1976 book *The Selfish Gene*,[5] which popularized a gene-centric[6] view of evolution. He builds on the concepts of natural selection and adaption, including in his analysis much of the work that was done in the century since Darwin that arrived at the hypothesis that evolution is focused on the gene rather than on the organism or even a group of organisms. Using terminology that has since become famous, Dawkins expressed this as the 'selfish gene'.

However, in the foreword to the book's 30th-anniversary edition, Dawkins said he 'can readily see that [the book's title] might give an inadequate impression of its contents' and in retrospect thinks he should have taken Tom Maschler's advice and called the book *The Immortal Gene*. The reason for his subsequent concern about the title is based on a misunderstanding that our genetic code causes us to be in conflict with each other and that selfless behaviour is an aberration.

---

[5] Drawing upon the 1966 work by the US evolutionary biologist George C. Williams in his book, *Adaptation and Natural Selection: A Critique of Some Current Evolutionary Thought*. This work hypothesized a gene-centric view of evolution.

[6] Dawkins definition of gene: A gene is defined as any form of chromosomal material that potentially lasts for enough generations to serve as a unit of natural selection (and to be distributed around in the form of copies).

The theory does hypothesize that species tend to evolve to maximize their potential or fitness for survival and that the number of copies collectively of its genes are a measure of its success in the evolutionary battleground. This implies that it is population as a whole that moves towards evolutionary stability and not particular individuals. On the contrary, from the gene-centred view, the more closely individuals are genetically related to each other, the more evolutionary sense it makes for selfless behaviour to occur.

The Selfish Gene states that gene selfishness is a fundamental principle of life and that this can explain both individual selfishness and individual altruism. In the mammalian world, with baboons that were studied by Dawkins for example, an individual is altruistic if he or she behaves in such a way as to increase another individual's welfare at the expense of his or her own. Selfish behaviour is the opposite. Dawkins goes further to say that some acts appear to be altruistic if looked at superficially, for they tend to make the altruistic person weaker and lower their own chances of survival, while helping someone else become more likely to survive. Even these acts are, when looked at closely, merely apparent altruism but are really disguised selfishness.

The essential argument is simple if one considers that evolution works at the lowest, the simplest level of all. Thus, the basic level of self-interest is not the species or an individual. It is the gene. If the gene is the basic unit of natural selection, and this view is not accepted by everyone,[7] then selfishness is but to be expected from it. Accepting that the gene is the basic unit, therefore, of selfishness, we must accept that at the genetic level, selfishness must be good and altruism bad.

We human beings, our individual bodies, to an evolutionary biologist are merely helping genes exist. We are their 'survival machines'. Nothing more!

---

[7] Some people regard the species as the unit of natural selection, others the population or group within the species, and yet others the individual.

Following this train of thought, each individual person is merely an agent for their genes, trying to propagate their genes and increase their number in the future. Naturally, it would be expected that the individual persons would also show altruistic and selfish behaviour towards each other. More selfish, if the genes had their way.

But luckily for us, we are not puppets being directly controlled by our genes. The genetic code sets up a pattern for us in advance, and then we are on our own. The genes cannot control us and are passive. It is a timing issue. Genes have slow reaction times as they work through control protein synthesis, which is exceedingly slow. Go watch paint dry for a thrill compared to the speed at which genes work. So, genes wind us up in advance, having taken a gamble at how we, and therefore the genes, will best survive in the world. They take the safe gambling decisions, the ones that show a pay-off in the long term. In the short term, genes have to sit by and watch us make our decisions as to how we live our lives. With human beings being particularly physically weak in a harsh world, the only survival mechanism our genes have given us through evolution is the ability to learn, the ability to simulate the future. Evolution of us as survival machines for our genes led us to consciousness. The evolutionary chain leading to human beings culminated in decision-making of such a level in the survival machines, in us, that we have almost wrested control from our genes. The genes are no longer our puppet masters. Our behaviour, selfish or altruistic or anything in between, is ultimately under the control of our genes through the central nervous system, but this is an indirect sort of control. The tables have been turned on the genes in fact. Instead of genes selecting the best survival machines, genes are themselves naturally selected by their ability to control effective decision-making survival machines. Evolution and natural selection means that genes need us to be independent thinkers.

It is when individuals start interacting in groups and communicating with each other that things start to get really interesting. At a genetic level, the only important communication between individuals is when one person influences the behaviour of another person. Discussions about the weather are purely frivolous and frowned upon by the great machines of evolution. Communication between individuals controlled by their individual genes must be mutually beneficial to both, else it would not occur at all. When you throw in natural selection and the fight for limited, if not scarce, resources, then there is conflict of interest. All communication between individuals contains, as a consequence, deception from the very beginning.

It is perhaps due to intuitive moral, spiritual and political beliefs that we hold on to group selection rather than accepting the battle of survival that genes are engaged in. The group-selection theory now commands little support within the ranks of professional evolutionary biologists, but it does appeal to social philosophers. At one extreme are theological arguments that one of the defining elements of a higher-order being, such as ourselves, is the willingness to sacrifice oneself for others. Other arguments support violent and aggressive behaviour, citing the need for only the fittest to survive.

There is no evidence that human beings, or any other living beings, evolve to meet some higher objective of enhancing the group or species. Perpetuation of the species is not the same thing as altruism.

In our finest moments, we admire those who sacrificed for others, who gave up for others. There are problem areas of course; a hero in a time of war is a mass murderer if the context were to be changed. Killing people outside war is one of the gravest crimes. Not so about killing other species. But the definition of 'us' and 'them', inherent in such discussions, is more deeply problematic. Nations are one 'group' for which altruistic and selfless behaviour is expected, but there are other groups from sports clubs and schools, to commercial unions and families. Altruism within a group very often becomes selfishness between groups. Should one save for one's family, or give away all one's surplus income every day to others who need it at that moment?

In the modern age, racial groupings and even deeply nationalistic identities are not favoured by the liberals. There is a move towards 'one humanity', and even the rights of the planet as a whole. The confusion is not about the big picture and the fuzzy, warm feeling we might get about the world marching in step towards a bright future. The dissonance is at what level we might expect altruism to occur, at the species, the nation, the family, or the individual level. Biology cannot answer this question, and neither can the theory of evolution. All that we know is that more closely are individuals related genetically, the more altruistic behaviour we can expect. Thus, families usually exhibit highly altruistic behaviour amongst themselves, until the seeming scarcity of resources causes family members to become selfish with each other. The existence of individual altruism still has to be explained.

The answer may lie beyond biology. It is not worth using analogies of the controversial and not widely accepted biological group selection to explain altruism and philanthropy. The need is for human behavioural sciences rather than biological sciences to provide the explanation. Critics of Dawkins argue that he only looks at the basic relationship from the selfish gene point of view, that we only engage in relationships in order to make our own genes go forward, the selfish gene. They argue that human beings work in groups. The former argument is biological, while the latter is about group dynamics. These are separate discussions. It is no doubt evident that human beings have consciousness, communicate and cooperate better than other species and that the relationships we build have resulted in the dominance of our species on the planet. But we cannot create analogies between evolutionary biology and psychological relationships between people.

Richard Dawkins does not make a philosophical statement that selfishness is desirable or that it is the guiding basis by which we should live. Neither does he make the argument that selfishness is inevitable. He makes a statistical biological argument that our genes, in their struggle for survival, build tendencies for self-preservation and, therefore, of selfishness. The selfish gene is not one single DNA strand! Altruism exists because we do not listen to our genes, because the behaviour of conscious, sentient human beings genes do not control our behaviour and the influence of genes can be overcome by social conditioning and other human interactions.

However, this does give us a warning. Our genes programme our initial behaviour, so in a sense we are born selfish. Society must teach philanthropy and altruism, because we may not be genetically programmed to be altruistic. We must teach our children to be charitable, generous and altruistic because it may not be part of the biology of their existence.

Social science steps in, as we shall see later in this book, to explain how collections of independent individual selfish entities might well combine to form supportive and altruistic societies. The selfish group without cooperation is doomed to be devoid of altruism, as it only focusses on the selfish exploitation of each other. With cooperation and consciousness emerge models of self-interest and altruism. Both evolutionary biology and social structures favouring stable cost–benefit analysis, using game-theoretical models and understanding human behaviour may shed light on individual philanthropy and altruism.

Last words on evolutionary biology come from the weird and counter-intuitive world of quantum mechanics. It has always been a mystery of how cellular structures can communicate with other cellular structures, in cases where neither physical material nor electromagnetic waves are passed between cells or other structures. The strange descriptions of life emerging from quantum biology might provide the explanation. There are the beginnings of hope that quantum biology may provide deeper insights into what life really is and provide answers to what is the 'soul' that gives life to lifeless bodies, and what is the 'spirit' that creates altruistic individuals, rather than selfish, struggling creatures.

Keira: 'I have applied as a volunteer to help young children in Africa. My friend from college told me about it. Isn't it a good idea?'

Rita: 'Undoubtedly noble. But in my view one doesn't have to go to Africa to make a difference, there is a lot that can be done here, in our local vicinity. Think about it'.

Keira: 'Sometimes you sound like my mother'.

Rita: 'Sometimes your mother can be right. Think about it'.

A SECOND CHANCE AT LIFE

Believe in yourself. You are braver than you think, more talented than you know, and capable of more than you imagine.
—Roy T. Bennett

Somashiv is nine years old and is in the third grade at school. He belongs to a small village town in Maharashtra called Nandumbar. It is a tribal village with little or no connectivity to the rest of the state and it lacks basic facilities. Somashiv is one of four children born to a poor couple. His mother, Kalabai, stays at home and looks after the children while her husband, Macchindra, is a farmer, who earns less than ₹3,000 a month, and that is when the crops do well. Macchindra looks up at the sky every morning to gauge what he calls the Mood of the Gods. His crop and therefore his livelihood depend on the weather and the crop cycle. Day after day, they struggle. There are six people to feed, and he is the only earning member of the family.

Somashiv was diagnosed with a CHD called a ventricular septal defect (VSD), which requires urgent closure with the use of a device specially designed for this delicate surgical intervention. In this condition, there is a hole between the lower chambers of the heart. Along with this, he was also suffering from pulmonary stenosis.

Somashiv was slow and became tired easily. No one in his family was aware that he was suffering from a heart disease until a government doctor visited the school and identified it. He was then evaluated further at an outreach Out Patient Department camp conducted by Jupiter Hospital in Shahada, two hours from his hometown, where he was advised surgery.

Kalabai and Macchindra were stumped by the complicated medical terminology, understanding little and terrified by the hospital. What they did understand, however, was that their Somashiv was very ill and terribly underweight.

His parents were scared, the neighbours counselled against it, and they had no one to turn to for advice. Being illiterate, they had to depend on the school for guidance.

Macchindra was under tremendous financial pressure. If he were to look after Somashiv, he would not be able to support the other children, because his meagre earning would not stretch to doing both. It would be a huge sacrifice if he were to try, but it was virtually impossible for him to put together the money needed for the surgery.

He surrendered to the will of God. To save one child he could not sacrifice the others. Every day he watched Somashiv grow weaker and struggled with his guilt. He decided to mortgage his fields to raise the money and even that, he was told, was not enough. But try he must. So, although the crop needed tending and he could not take time off to travel to Mumbai, since Somashiv's condition now needed a big hospital, he still went. The logistics of getting Somashiv to Mumbai, the language barrier, and many other impediments slowed them down, making it impossible for them to even begin the journey to Jupiter Hospital in Mumbai. However, with the help of a local doctor they managed to arrange the travel and took Somashiv to Mumbai for treatment.

The procedure, upon evaluation, required closure with balloon pulmonary valvotomy, which included closing the hole with a device and opening the blocked valve with balloon dilation. This procedure was extremely challenging due to the remote location of the hole within the heart. It would take nearly five hours, whereas a routine straightforward VSD closure takes not more than 45 minutes.

And the cost would be equally magnified. But someone was listening, and a group of philanthropists funded the operation.

Those five hours were the longest and most difficult for Macchindra. He sat huddled alone in the hospital, feeling totally lost amongst the jostling crowds in a big city hospital. As he sat there, he was racked by guilt. Had he delayed the surgery? Would it lead to more problems? What would he tell his wife and other children? He felt weighed down and very alone in the crowded hospital.

Finally, the doctors came up to him and told him that not only had the surgery been successful but also that there were no complications.

Macchindra broke into tears. His loud sobs could be heard down the corridor; it had been nerve-wracking and the sheer relief of knowing that his child was well was too much for him. He turned around to embrace the embarrassed doctor, who patted him on the shoulder understanding the rush of emotion.

Somashiv's recovery took place at a brilliant pace. He was walking and eating the same day and discharged from hospital within two days. Grinning mischievously, he waved goodbye when led out of the hospital by his father.

He resumed school soon after. Somashiv loves school; he is doing well despite having missed a lot of school due to ill health

His father, like any other parent, wants him to study well and live a healthy life. He believes that his son has been granted a second life and must make the most of it. He never tires of telling Somashiv this, urging him to study hard. 'Be someone and do some good', he tells him. 'Believe in yourself because very few are given a second chance at life and living', he tells Somashiv every morning as the boy dresses for school.

For the group of altruists who reached out, Somashiv will always be special. He was the first child from the tribal belt that they could help, and it means that their work is reaching people who have little access to medical care and that it is making a difference even in areas totally cut off from mainstream India.

3

ORIGINS OF ALTRUISM MEME

The secret of getting ahead is getting started.
—Sally Berger

Ask any non-reclusive teenager about a 'meme' and you will get vigorous nods of the familiar. The 'meme', a cultural or social idea transmitted virally, often through electronic media is all pervasive in the world of the under-20s, and increasingly being adopted by popular cultures of all ages. Memes are often pictorial and intended to be satires, humorous or to ridicule public behaviour. Some memes have deeper meaning, intending to convey serious thoughts and concepts. This social phenomenon is worldwide and seems to display two characteristics. It spreads quickly from person to person and it replicates itself as it travels.

Memes existed before electronic media took over much of social communication in the world. A meme was an idea, a concept, a human cultural unit that could spread through replicating itself.

Drawing an analogy from the gene concept, Richard Dawkins coined the neologism, 'meme',[8] as:

> A meme is an idea, behaviour, or style that spreads from person to person within a culture. A meme acts as a unit for carrying cultural ideas, symbols, or practices that can be transmitted from one mind to another through writing, speech, gestures, rituals, or other imitable phenomena with a mimicked theme. Supporters of the concept regard memes as cultural analogues to genes in that they self-replicate, mutate, and respond to selective pressures.

Transmission of human culture, the central feature of humanity, is analogous to genetic transmission. There is replication and reproduction, two important elements of evolution, and similar concepts of natural selection by looking for stable equilibria. The gene and evolutionary biology, as we saw earlier, cannot be the sole basis for understanding human behaviour or even evolution. Memes are the unit of cultural transmission. The human beings we are today is not merely a function of our genes; it is also a function of the memes we have created for ourselves.

Many of the deepest ideas of our culture are memes. The idea of God, economic structures such as money or capitalism, tribes such as football or cricket teams, and the concepts of altruism and philanthropy are memes. And memes replicate through imitation. They are transmitted through human communication; the spoken and written word, personal example and so on.

Most physicists would agree that most of what Isaac Newton said is wrong in detail, yet it provides a working model of the world for those who understand his work. A meme of Newton's laws

---

[8] Richard Dawkins took the Ancient Greek word 'mimeme'—meaning 'imitated thing'—and shortened it to 'meme'.

exists in the heads of most of those who went through formal schooling. And despite being, in detail, wrong, Newton's laws work very well for the most part of our existence.[9]

True philanthropy and generosity may be another meme, a quality of human beings that prevents the selfishness of the genes from acting upon the behaviour of individuals. Cultivating altruism and social togetherness may well be what differentiates not just human beings from other animals on the planet, but also *Homo sapiens* from all other human beings that have walked the earth.

Harari (2015) identifies the Cognitive Revolution about 70,000 years ago[10] as having been the origin of human history and the birth of *Homo sapiens*. Of the many human species that inhabited the earth, the dominance of our species lies in the way we think and communicate. We have created memes for Gods, nations, human rights, money, laws, bureaucracy, and philanthropy. From the early beginnings of social organization were born human cultures.

The Cognitive Revolution came about through the coming together of a set of happy circumstances, at least for us *Homo sapiens*. We, as a species, could have become extinct, could have died out without leaving a trace on the earth. Instead, we emerged as the dominant species on the planet, able to be social and to discuss altruism amongst ourselves.

Human beings were weak and helpless compared with other creatures. But we had a fundamentally defining characteristic, in

---

[9] While Newton's theories were excellent for describing the motions of bodies on Earth or in space accurately in the late 17th century, closer inspection of the motion of stellar bodies reveals shortcomings. Newton's Laws of Motion are approximations that we work with, but these are incorrect in detail. There is still a place to talk about the historical development of the interaction between forces and matter, and Newton played a large role here (as did Aristotle and Galileo). Einstein, in his general theory of relativity, was the first to successfully improve on the gravitational theories of Newton.

[10] Humans first emerged in East Africa around 2.5 million years ago, having evolved from an earlier species of apes.

that we had considerably larger brains than any other animals had. Further, the young ones of most other animals were born able to cope with nature and life in a relatively short span of time, some almost immediately on birth. Human babies continue to be almost entirely dependent upon adults for years for food, shelter and protection. The learning of human babies is rapid in the early years, but not of a kind that aids survival at a young age. The social instinct was born from the need for adult human beings to gather around and protect their young ones. And this could not be done alone in the time of the hunter-gatherers. It required adults other than the mother to help raise a human child. The saying 'it takes a village to raise a child' could not have been truer!

The fact that human beings survived and became the dominant species is evidence that evolution worked in favour of those characteristics and individuals who could form social bonds and tribal instincts. The brain developed further, but cognition also gave the unique ability for human beings to educate their young ones in abstract ideas. The memes we referred to earlier were a direct consequence of evolution leading to thinking, cognitive human beings, able to socialize and to educate their children. Rationalization of our reality post the event of our dominance runs in an argument of this form: random mutations in the genetic code changed the way the neurons in our brains were wired, leading to amazing cognitive skills and different ways of communication. This, in turn, created the Cognitive Revolution.

Harari identified that

> the period from about 70,000 years ago to about 30,000 years ago witnessed the invention of boats, oil lamps, bows and arrows and needles (essential for sewing warm clothing). The first objects that can reliably be called art date from this era, as does the first clear evidence for religion, commerce, and social stratification. Most researchers believe that these unprecedented accomplishments were the product of a revolution in Sapiens' cognitive abilities.

Yet, cognition was not enough. It also required the special ability of language and communication that human beings developed. All human languages have the ability to describe and communicate limitless subtle variations of the world around us and countless unique meanings, from a simple base of finite, limited language structures. One of the greatest wonders of the world is that a small group of sounds produced by our physically limited vocal cords and heard by our equally limited ears, can lead to the richness of thought, cognition and communication that human beings possess.

Brain rather than brawn was the reason human beings survived to later dominate the planet. But we have not been satisfied with mere survival and reproduction, which might have been enough for our selfish genes. We have gone further, not merely in developing the abstractions that are unique to human beings, but also in developing social structures so intense that gossip and discussion have moved well beyond survival and reproduction.

Human needs and wants are not at a base survival level any more ... the social relationships and well-being of humans require greater sustenance. And being supremely social animals, the instinct of herding others to reach these higher levels of living are in-bred into us. Therefore, human beings act as social tribes in their altruistic behaviour, not being content merely with each individual having basic food, security and shelter. We have even created memes such as Human Rights, which lay out the human-given 'right' for every person of our species to be able to survive, live with adequate food and security, and have the ability to bring up their young ones in shelter and with support. This Bill of Rights does not even begin to have space in the minds of other animals on the planet.

Even animals that have complicated communication patterns find it impossible to gossip and communicate about inane matters. Talking behind people's backs, speaking about what does not really matter, gossiping ... these might seem like frivolous activities in the serious world we live in, but these were the very characteristics that have led to the absolute dominance of our species. Who said that evolution worked in boring ways!

The essential feature was that this social animal, the human being, had the ability to cooperate, through social structures and language that became increasingly complicated as the number of people in a tribe grew from a few tens to many thousands and beyond. Cooperation in these large numbers, and in the millions of humans who inhabit the earth today, seems to depend upon the ability to gossip.

Do not, however, be misled into thinking that gossip rules the world! Gossip has its limitations, so human beings invented elaborate structures and memes for social organization. Harari claims that research evidence indicates a maximum group size of 150 persons who can be closely bound together by gossip. The social structures of the human world are far bigger than that, reaching to mega sizes in the interconnected world economy or in organized religion. Small communities can still be organized informally, but larger groups need formal structures, hierarchies and titles. This will have a critical impact on our understanding of how altruistic behaviour actually works with different groupings of people.

As communication and our language developed, human beings were able not merely to talk about descriptions of the world around them, but also to create ideas about things that did not really exist outside their imagination. Magic, science and religion were born out of myths, stories and imagination. This imagination helped us question 'why' the world exists, where we came from, what will happen next … and enabled us to become even better as social animals. Alone in all living beings on earth, our minds gave us the ability to cooperate and work together as large populations, including with relative or complete strangers who broadly followed the same set of rules as we did. Money, for instance, is a meme created by human beings, but the economic and commercial transactions of the world would come to a grinding halt if this meme were not truly believed by unconnected and unrelated persons across the world. It is these common myths, memes, that have allowed large groups of virtual strangers to collaborate across our world. Other living things collaborate from time to time, but only in local areas and only for immediate or closely connected goals. Human beings are able to collaborate widely, and one of the roots of altruism stems from this ability.

This web of tales, myths and stories is so ingrained in us that we do not even consider them to be memes at all. The legal system, human rights, world trade and commerce, the structure of firms and corporations, the schooling system and curriculum, driving rules, governments and the United Nations. All of these are inventions of the human mind ... and incredibly powerful inventions. The meme is perhaps stronger than the gene in creating human dominance on the planet.

Importantly, the stories can change. Sometimes individuals can change the narrative, and at other times it is the larger groups of people who do so. Franklin Marshall wrote a moving book about Louden Nelson, a slave who gave his house to save the only school in Santa Cruz, California, in 1860 just before he died. Other than Nelson's belief that his past would not be his future and that he would change his narrative, the true story has an even more moving ending. Marshall used Nelson's story in 2003 when two schools in Santa Cruz City were closing for lack of money. Nearly a century and a half after he died, Nelson became a story, a meme that people could believe in. Collective philanthropy and governmental lobbying led to US$6.5 million being raised, and the two schools were kept open.

'Nearly all Americans live comfortably', said Alexis de Tocqueville in his 1835 book *Democracy in America*, and yet 'in America, there are few rich'. The wealthy, he continued, 'are few and powerless; they have no privileges that attract public observation; even their wealth, as it is no longer incorporated and bound up with the soil, is impalpable and, as it were, invisible'.

Andrew Carnegie was born that year. At the close of the 19th century, Carnegie gave away most of the immense wealth he had achieved to charity and philanthropic causes. The estimated US$350 million he gave would today be worth about five billion. While this was an individual action, it was part of a meme of his generation, where the richest American business leaders, from

Carnegie to Rockefeller, Vanderbilt, Sears and Ford, created the tradition of American large-scale giving, of American philanthropy. These industry leaders and philanthropists were also maligned and criticized, even to the extent of being called Robber Barons.[11] These men were criticized for being corrupt and exploitative of workers. Their complex story, their meme, changed from exploitation to that of giving.

More than a hundred years later, the debate is no longer about capitalism, socialism, workers' rights or how the Robber Barons made their money. The arguments are about the role of self-directed philanthropy, as handled by the great philanthropists of their time and since, versus the social-welfare role of the state, the government. The beauty of the human mind and the stories we create is that once the central meme is that of 'helping one's fellow human being', we can continue to argue the merits and demerits of the mechanism, but we do not need to discuss the idea of altruism any more.

'It is not from the benevolence of the butcher, the brewer, or the baker that we expect our dinner, but from their regard to their own interest', said Adam Smith, referring to self-interest driving philanthropy as if by an 'invisible hand'. Whatever be the motivation, and we shall discuss some of this later in the book, altruism was here to stay.

Once created in the complex network of human stories, memes such as altruism exist and accumulate power. Whether these are 'social constructs' or 'imagined realties' is beside the point. These are not lies. As Harari says, 'Unlike lying, an imagined reality is something that everyone believes in, and as long as this communal belief persists, the imagined reality exerts force in the world'.

---

[11] The term 'robber baron' derives from the Raubritter or robber knights. These medieval German lords charged nominally illegal tolls unauthorized by the Holy Roman Emperor on the primitive roads crossing their lands or larger tolls along the Rhine river. They lined their pockets at the cost of the common good without adding anything of value.

Human beings live in a dual world of reality. One is the 'real' world of objective reality of what exists around us, and the other is the 'imagined' world of the memes and ideas that drive our species.

Essentially, therefore, human beings outstripped other species in their ability to gossip, cooperate, create social structures and invent elaborate memes to rule their reality, often changing the memes as they were no longer useful. For the rest of the living world, the selfish gene continued to rule. Human beings outstripped the influence of their genes, to create a reality that had as much to do with the Cognitive Revolution as it had to do with evolutionary biology. This is not to presume that human beings are not subject to natural laws and biology; we live and die just as other living beings do. It is that we have created an alternate reality within the framework of life.

Later in this book, we will look at how the humanities and social sciences try to explain exactly how the imagined order is woven into the tapestry of life. Altruism is now embedded into our world. Although it began as an imagined reality, it is part of the material world we live in. This imagined reality shapes what we expect, what we desire, our needs, wants and group dynamics. Collective actions are guided by the imagined reality, the meme, of altruism and of helping fellow human beings. This does not mean that there is always agreement on what altruism means or what mechanisms are most useful in helping others. There is often violent disagreement between the role of the state and that of individuals, of whether social order and welfare are best directed by well-intentioned people, communities or the government. However, this Cognitive Dissonance, along with the ability to hold paradoxically divergent views in one's head at the same time, is one of the strengths of human beings. 'Had people been unable to hold contradictory beliefs and values, it would probably have been impossible to establish and maintain any human culture', says Harari.

There is a last aspect that must be considered in tracing the origins of the altruism meme. Adam Smith, in his book *The Wealth of Nations*, made the argument that it is the selfish human urge to increase private profit that is the basis for collective wealth. He said that effectively greed and becoming richer helped not just the businessman but also everyone else. Egoistical behaviour leads to altruism, as it is only in the surplus from economic activity that charity and philanthropy can flourish.

Keira: 'My friend says there is a right time for everything. She wants to get a good job, earn well, marry better and when her children grow up, she will do social service and give'.

Rita: 'Do the small things first, give as you grow. Don't wait for the big moment because life is a journey and our wants change with our goalposts. We may never find the right moment'.

A LIVING MIRACLE

So comes snow after fire, and even dragons have their endings.
—J. R. R. Tolkien

This is a story about a little girl, hearing of whom will make one grateful for the privileges that we take for granted. Hearing her story is difficult, because the pain and abject poverty that she has seen makes one cringe, and her situation could have cost the little girl her life.

Reema is an 11-year-old girl from Thrissur district in Kerala. She was born in March 2007, to a low-income Malayali family. She has an older sister, Amrita. Her father is the only earning member of the family and works as a driver in Delhi. Her parents, Dinesh and Amu, were extremely happy to welcome her into their small family, but their joy soon turned to worry as they noticed their newborn daughter turn blue. To their absolute horror, she was breathless and gasped for air often. Feeding her was a nightmare and she cried all the time.

They were devastated when doctors at the AIIMS, New Delhi, diagnosed a complex cyanotic CHD that was difficult to treat and needed multiple complicated heart surgeries. Reema was born with an extremely rare heart disorder where her heart was on the right side (dextrocardia) instead of being on the left. All chambers of her heart were in an extremely unusual location; the ventricles were one-on-top-of-the-other (superioinferior) instead of being left-and-right; both great arteries arose from her superiorly positioned right ventricle (double outlet right ventricle); there were two large holes (VSDs); and her pulmonary artery (which carries impure blood to lungs) was severely obstructed. As a result, she had very low oxygen levels at all times.

Her unusual and complex condition meant that she would need a series of heart operations, which would naturally be expensive. Amu and Dinesh could not afford the treatment and were completely devastated.

With financial support from the Amritanandamayi Math and AIIMS, she underwent the first emergency operation in 2007 (BT shunt), and subsequently a second palliative operation in 2010 (Glenn shunt). These surgeries extended her life beyond childhood.

However, the worst was not over. As Reema grew older, she became progressively more breathless and turned blue more often. However, due to the complex nature of her surgery and the expenses and logistical problems involved, further operations were delayed.

The doctors did not give up on her. Harnessing the power of technology, the doctors at AIIMS used 3D printing to create a 3D replica of her heart. This allowed them to understand her rare and complex problems better. Using the 3D model, the doctors were able to meticulously plan her next round of surgery.

The heavily discounted surgery would still cost almost ₹300,000, a princely sum for the impoverished family. Her parents gave up; it was impossible for them to raise the money and yet watching her die a little every day was torturous.

Temples and fakirs, the village soothsayer—none could alleviate their sense of despair. 'Why me? Why us?' asked Amu, and her husband had no answer for her.

Every day Dinesh left for work hoping for a miracle but returned empty-handed. His employers turned him down, banks would not let him in since he had little to pledge against a loan. His wife's little jewellery, which meant so much to them, had little value in the real world.

And just when he despaired and lost hope, life looked up. For they say the darkest hour is just before the breaking of dawn.

His employer called a charitable foundation, who came forward and agreed to fund a significant proportion of the expenses for the child's surgery. This initial funding empowered the family to take the tough decision, a decision to go ahead with the extremely difficult and complicated operation.

Reema was finally operated upon at AIIMS in July 2018 by the leading AIIMS paediatric surgical team. The surgery was a success, and she is now recovering well.

Through both surgeries, one of her uncle's, her mother and father stood by her bedside, ensuring Reema was surrounded by love and support.

Reema is much better and she is back at school. Her friends never tire of asking her about the operation. And she shows her scars with pride. After all, it is her story to tell, one in which she is the heroine and the team of doctors along with the altruists are the heroes.

She play-acts the entire situation and talks about the big hospital, which only she has seen from amongst all those in her school. Her teachers encourage her studies by paying extra attention to her. Several of them voluntarily coached her so that she could catch up with her work. The principal of her school describes her as a warm and talkative young girl, popular with children her age.

Despite her health issues, Reema remains positive about life. She is protective of her sister, but at the same time does not think twice while ticking her off when she is naughty.

She waits for her father to get home so that she can grab his mobile phone and then hide it, giggling as she watches him look for it. Like other children her age, with a mobile in her hand, homework is forgotten. She can spend hours playing games. Ask her about the latest apps and she will surprise even tech gurus with her range of information.

Reema often says that in the virtual world, her heart beats the same way as others, and she can forget the pain and discomfort.

Her parents take her regularly and follow the medical regime and post-operative care prescribed by the doctors. For her parents, she is a living miracle. Each time they see her smile, they know that sometimes life works itself out. And that when all is lost, hope still exists. As they say, magic happens when you do not give up even if everything around you is going wrong. For the universe, they say, always falls in love with a stubborn heart.

Reema exemplifies this spirit of endurance, of not giving up. Her doctors told her parents that it was her holding on to hope that she will get better that made their task easier. For patients who give up despite the best medical treatment often succumb. So, medicine and hope have the power to heal.

Reema and her family continue to live in Delhi but feel more settled now. And Reema and her sister have adopted a stray dog, Kaalu, who follows them everywhere.

4

THE GAME THEORY OF GIVING

I believe that words are easy. I believe that the truth is told in actions we take. And I believe that if enough ordinary people back up our desire for a better world with action, I believe we can, in fact, accomplish absolutely extraordinary things.
—Jody Williams

Charities do not always generate an economic surplus through their normal activities, and most charities require external funding to be effective. Some, of course, are grant-endowed and use the returns from investment of that grant to fund their activities, while others perform some commercial functions and cross subsidize their philanthropic activities. Funds, as we will use the term, are sums of money or other resources whose principal or interest is set apart for a specific objective. A significant proportion of charity funding comes from individuals. Therefore, it is imperative for charities to understand what motivates people to donate. We now examine the economic reasons behind donations, even when the act appears counter-intuitive. The game-theoretic approach is used to analyse the interplay of self-interest and public service involved in acts of altruism, and specifically in the act of donating for philanthropic or charitable purposes. We will also examine the 'warm glow' effect that could arise from prosocial behaviour[12] and could result in the donor receiving a positive pay-off and explain the effect of this positive pay-off in the form of a coordination game model. Finally, we look at the impact of this game theory analysis on the fundraising strategies used by charities.

Before going any further, it is important to understand in simple terms what game theory actually is. Game theory is the formal study of conflict and cooperation. Game-theoretic concepts apply whenever the actions of several agents are interdependent. These agents may be individuals, groups, firms or any combination of these. The concepts of game theory provide a language to formulate, structure, analyse and understand strategic scenarios. It is a tool that analyses and allows for strategic decision-making.

Economists have often spoken about the idea of 'Homo economicus', or a human that made rational decisions purely based on self-interest. In game theory, making decisions based on self-interest generally refers to making decisions such that the individual's pay-off is maximized. It is natural to assume that a purely self-interested player would be averse to donating, though we have seen hints in an earlier chapter of how this self-interest is balanced by our social behaviour as hums. This is because giving money without getting a direct material benefit in return might be seen as a negative pay-off rather than a positive one. However, this line of reasoning is too simplistic in its nature. It fails to consider the fact that pay-offs can be defined in different ways, many of which are non-monetary in nature.

Evidence suggests that people do indeed donate large amounts of money in cash and in kind, year after year. According to the

---

[12] 'Prosocial behaviour' is any action intended to help others. One motivation for prosocial behaviour is altruism or the desire to help others with no expectation of reward.

World Giving Index (2013), around 50 to 60 per cent of households in the developed world choose to give to charity.

Though monetary pay-offs are not usually attained in return, there are other factors that motivate people to donate. Olson (1965) stated:

> Economic incentives are not, to be sure, the only incentives; people are sometimes also motivated by a desire to win prestige, respect, friendship, and other social and psychological objectives ... The possibility that, in a case where there was no economic incentive for an individual to contribute to the achievement of a group interest, there might nonetheless be a social incentive for him to make such a contribution, must therefore be considered.

Thus, when people make donations to privately provided public goods, such as charity, social pressure, guilt, sympathy or simply a desire for a 'warm glow' may play important roles in the decisions of agents (Andreoni 1990). Warm glow refers to prosocial behaviour that causes the actor to experience positive feelings, apart from its social implications (Evren and Minardi 2017).

Since the 1980s, dozens of experiments have tested whether selfish benefits are enough to explain altruistic behaviour. In an intervention by Sheldon and Lyubomirsky in 2004, US university students were asked to perform five random acts of kindness per week, over the course of six weeks. Such acts were described as 'behaviours that benefit others' or 'make others happy', typically at some cost to oneself (e.g., dropping coins into a stranger's parking meter, donating blood, helping a friend with a problem set, visiting a sick relative or writing a thank-you note to a former teacher). A no-treatment control group was also part of the experiment. This group did not perform any acts of kindness. Both groups completed questionnaires measuring well-being; first, immediately before the intervention and, last, immediately after the intervention. Their findings showed that while the control group experienced a reduction in happiness over the course of the six-week period, the experimental group experienced an increase. This experiment provided greater credibility to the theory that doing good does lead to positive feelings or the 'warm glow' referred to earlier.

In another experiment, researchers approached individuals of the same university, handed them a US$5 or US$20 bill, and then randomly assigned them to spend the money on themselves or on others by the end of the day. When participants were contacted that evening, individuals who had been assigned to spend their windfall on others were happier than those who had been assigned to spend the money on themselves (Dunn et al. 2008). Interestingly, the amount of money that participants received (US$5 or US$20) did not influence happiness levels, suggesting that how people spent their money was more important than how much money they spent.

These experiments do, indeed, seem to provide direct support to the causal argument that spending money on others promotes happiness or has a warm glow effect. However, it may be argued that people are likely to claim that they experienced an increase in happiness when they spent on others, even if they did not. This could be caused by social-desirability bias, or the need to feel that doing the 'right' thing is important.

But evidence of happiness experienced by individuals engaging in prosocial spending goes beyond reported claims. Subjects in an experiment underwent functional magnetic resonance imaging (fMRI) while they played a dictator game. Subjects received US$100 and then made decisions about whether or not to give money to a local food bank. The experiment showed that both voluntary and mandatory donations led to activation in brain areas typically associated with receiving rewards (Harbaugh et al. 2007). Therefore, scientific experiments too provide credibility to the warm glow phenomenon.

A subsequent investigation also found that this positive relationship between prosocial spending and happiness is not restricted to specific regions or income groups. In this investigation, the responses of over 230,000 participants drawn from 142 countries in the Gallup World Poll (Aknin et al. 2013). Respondents reported their overall well-being and whether they had donated money to charity in the past month. The relationship between prosocial spending and well-being was positive in 127 out of 142 countries around the world, even after controlling for individuals' household income. Additionally, the relationship was unrelated to the average income of each country, suggesting that donating money to charity has emotional benefits in rich and poor countries alike.

The experiments above establish that it is indeed possible for there to be positive utility to be derived from prosocial behaviour, due to the warm glow effect. However, it is important to note that just because warm glow can be derived from prosocial behaviour does not imply that it is always derived. There are people who do not derive warm glow from prosocial behaviour.

Analysing using game theory, let us say that someone who gets a warm glow from donating is 'warm' and someone who does not is 'cold'. A 'cold' person would rather not donate, regardless of the success of the charity, as he would not derive any warm glow from donating. Conversely, a 'warm' person would want to donate if the charity is a project as he would derive warm glow from donating. However, both the 'cold' and the 'warm' people would rather not have donated if the project fails. Kahneman and Tversky (1982) explained that if the consequences of an action are positive, people feel much happier from having acted than if the consequences are negative and the same result occurs.

To put in game theory terms:

1. 'Not donate' is the dominant strategy for the 'cold' person (player 1) as he is better off not donating, regardless of whether the charity project succeeds

2. For the 'warm' person (player 2), there are two possibilities:

   A. Everyone else donated: The project is a success, and therefore the last person would also want to donate and benefit from warm glow

   B. No one else donates: The project fails, and therefore the last person is better off not donating

3. In game theory, there are two pure-strategy Nash equilibria:[13] Either everyone donates or no one donates; this is a coordination game.

A specific example, in game theory terms, is given below:

1. For the 'warm' person (player 1), there are two possibilities:

   A. Everyone else donated: The project is a success, and therefore the last person would also want to donate and benefit from warm glow. We take the positive utility derived by player 1 from donating to a successful charity as 10 utils.

   B. No one else donates: The project fails, and therefore the last person is better off not donating. We take the negative utility to player 1 upon donating to an unsuccessful charity as (−)5 utils.

2. 'Not donate' is the dominant strategy for the 'cold' person (player 2) as he is better off not donating, regardless of whether the charity project succeeds. He receives no satisfaction from donating, and thus the utility derived in all scenarios is 0.

3. There are two pure-strategy Nash equilibrium: Either everyone donates or no one donates; this is a coordination game.

---

[13] Nash equilibrium, in economics and game theory, is a stable state of a system involving the interaction of different participants, in which no participant can gain by a unilateral change of strategy if the strategies of the others remain unchanged.

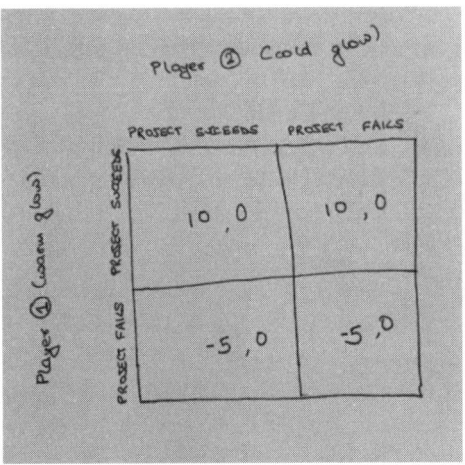

Since the 'cold' people would receive no pay-off regardless of the success of the charity, we focus on the 'warm' people. The takeaway for charities from this demonstration is that to get 'warm' people to donate, it is important to show them that the charity's project is likely to succeed.

There is also another takeaway for charities. If 'warm' people are the ones who donate, it would follow that the more the 'warm' people, the greater is the number of donors. But how could charities help in increasing the number of 'warm' people? One potential method has been discussed below.

The premise is that just because this warm glow effect exists so prevalently does not mean that people are always aware of it. Dunn et al. (2014), while surveying students from the University of British Columbia in Canada, found that a significant majority erroneously assume that spending money on themselves would make them happier than spending on others. This showed that people are not always aware of the warm glow effect or the happiness that they derive from prosocial spending.

The question that arises is whether making people aware of the happiness derived from charitable donations would incentivize people to donate more. It is known that tampering with intrinsic behaviours could be detrimental. If a person is rewarded for performing an activity, his intrinsic motivation could decrease (Gneezy and Rustichini 2000).

Anik et al. (2009) investigated whether advertising the mood benefits of charitable acts change the motivations and outcomes of donating. In an initial test of this question, a sample of over 1,000 readers of *The New York Times*, who had just read about research demonstrating the link between giving and happiness, were asked to answer questions about their personal and prosocial spending and their well-being. It was found that respondents who reported having spent more that day on others reported greater happiness, whereas there was no relationship between spending on oneself and happiness. Therefore, making people aware of the warm glow derived from prosocial spending did not cause their happiness associated from donations to diminish. A potential area for further study is whether this awareness of emotional benefits of donations could lead to an increase in the amount of donations.

Many charities seem to believe that it does, for they have adopted the 'feel-good strategy' to encourage donations. The American Red Cross, for instance, tells prospective blood donors that 'the need is constant. The gratification is instant'. Andreoni (1995) pointed out that the effect of the asymmetry between positive and negative externalities may be seen in the actions of fundraisers and in the advertisements of charitable organizations. It seems much more common to hear appeals of the virtue that one's contribution will make rather than to the tragedies that will occur if a contribution is not made. Some even appeal directly to the good feeling to be had by contributing. If such a positive–negative asymmetry exists, it may have taught fundraisers that positive appeals are more productive in generating contributions to public goods.

Other ways of increasing donations involve addressing the social concerns that underlie the warm glow. In other words, charities could increase the number of 'warm' people, thereby increasing the donations they receive. Jasper and Samek (2014) outline a few such methods in their study.

One strategy is that of the Demonstration Effect. Charities provide information about past donations, thereby making potential donors feel part of a community and reinforcing the positive social feeling that might come from donating, and thereby adding to the warm glow felt by people. This approach is backed by research. Jasper and Samek (2014) describe how Frey and Meier conducted a field experiment with university students in which some students were randomized to receive information that a large proportion of other students had donated to the fund in the previous year, while others were randomized to receive information that a small proportion of other students had donated. The study found that students receiving information that many students had donated earlier were more likely to donate themselves. Shang and Croson (2009) conducted a field experiment as part of a radio fundraising campaign, informing those who called in about the past donations of others. The researchers found that information given to potential donors about large gifts from others increased contribution amounts, while information about small gifts decreased contribution amounts.

The clear takeaway for charities from research and anecdotal evidence is that charities should include examples of past donations in their campaigns to increase the number of 'warm' people donating.

A second potential strategy for charities is the Visibility Effect. Experience of fundraising has shown that increasing the visibility of donations can be a key motivator for giving. Individuals who are recognized for their efforts may be more likely to donate. As advanced by Vesterlund (2003), two theories underlie the effectiveness of this approach. First, donors may experience an increase in utility from an improved social image. Second, donors may wish to signal to others the importance of donating. Research testing the assumption and discriminating between anonymity and visibility in donations was conducted by Soetevent (2005) by randomly assigning churches to pass around open or closed collection baskets. Open baskets increased contributions, but the positive effect declined over time. Further evidence from other research indicated that social image may play a larger role than immediate visibility for oneself. A field experiment allowed potential donors to give using cash or debit cards, where debit card donations were more visible to person asking for the gift, but cash was obviously more apparent to giver and those around the giver. The study found that debit card donations led to fewer, but larger gifts.

The use of online and electronic social media to generate visibility was investigated for its impact of incentivizing donors to post online about their donations. Incentives increased the likelihood of posting, and resulted in increased new donations for the charity, indicating a positive impact of this strategy. The Visibility Effect, therefore, is yet another strategy that uses the 'warm glow' concept, by harnessing an improved social image to increase donations.

In conclusion, the warm glow theory offers an explanation as to why people donate, despite the act seeming counter-intuitive. This warm glow is affected by factors such as social image. It can lead to prosocial behaviour having a positive not negative pay-off, and thus making strategic sense according to game theory. However, not all people derive warm glow from the act of giving. Thus, it is important for charities to understand what causes the warm glow effect and to use this to enhance their fundraising projects. Social concerns often underlie the warm glow. Giving tends to increase when social distance is reduced, when people communicate, or when the recipient is identified specifically rather than statistically.

Warm glow charity has often been contrasted with altruistic behaviour. There are people who, regardless of outcome, wish to do good. Recent studies have tried to figure out how this good can be maximized in the most efficient way. There is, for instance, a tendency to prefer forms of giving that involve significant sacrifice and effort, such as running marathons (or taking the ice-bucket challenge). This is often ineffective but has a tremendous 'feel-good' factor. Donations may have a bigger impact, and the challenge for charities is to balance the outreach of 'feel-good' events, with effective targeting of donors.

Keira: 'My father gave money to his relatives and they cheated him. I don't like giving money. I give other things'.

After a pause.

Keira: 'I earn a small salary, so I give little. I do my bit. But you earn more, so shouldn't you give more?'

Rita: 'That is not how it works, give what you can sustain, do your bit, be the change'.

'Did you know that people give for different reasons? Some choose to remain anonymous?'

THE DAUGHTER WITH GOLDEN SMILE

Despite the forecast, live it like it's spring.
—Lilly Pulitzer

Tamil Nadu is a state in South India. Sridevi was born in Tamil Nadu. Her parents, Rani and Ramamoorthy, were overjoyed when they welcomed her into this world along with their extended family. She was the first girl born to their generation, and unlike many others, her birth was celebrated.

In India, the birth of a daughter is still considered a scourge. Many babies do not live to celebrate their first birthday. Stories about infant girls a few days old no longer make headlines. Rani and Ramamoorthy are different. They had prayed for the birth of a child, specifically a girl child. Having lost his sister recently, Ramamoorthy felt his sister's presence in his newborn daughter. His happiness was infectious, and his wife smiled as the baby was given to her.

However, their joy was short-lived. When the baby was eight days old, she had to be rushed to hospital, and the doctors gave them news that reduced them to tears. They were not able to grasp the full implication of what was being said, but they did understand that their baby was very ill.

She had been diagnosed with 'd-TGA', a CHD in which the two main arteries of the heart switch position. She required a switch operation, which could be done at the Amrita Institute of Medical Sciences in Kochi, but the parents didn't have enough money to meet the cost of surgery and other expenses associated with the medical treatment.

Parents of small children born with severe illness often suffer from anxiety, depression and suicidal thoughts. And if, to top that, there are financial problems, then all of the above get exacerbated. This is a true story, one in which hope and despair can be found in equal measure but with a difference. The child survives.

Ramamoorthy was a salesman. The emotional turmoil of a sick child resulted in his dismissal from his job. This plunged the family into despair and hopelessness. All seemed to be lost, and their life seemed to be caving in. On the one hand, the lost job meant immediate paucity of funds and, on the other, the mounting medical expenditures meant they had the burden of unrepayable loans.

He was absolutely stunned. Life had tripped him; the happiest week in his life had morphed into a nightmare. It was as if the life he had known before the birth of his child belonged to someone else. He spent hours pacing his modest home, carrying the baby who wheezed constantly and cried incessantly. Her breathing was laboured, and it broke his heart.

Rani was beside herself with grief and cried incessantly. The problems seemed even larger because she was weak from post-delivery complications. Ramamoorthy and his mother were looking after the baby at the time. Rani was still in hospital, recovering after the delivery.

They had no income, and the operation to save the baby was imperative. 'No time to be lost if you want to save her', the doctors had told them in no uncertain words.

They were left with no choice but to borrow money from family and close friends. With all the support that they got, they managed to put together ₹100,000, gathered from people who themselves could ill afford to lend the money, knowing that it may never be returned.

Ramamoorthy went to the doctor with the money he had collected, it just wasn't enough. Looking into the doctor's eyes, he appealed for help to save his daughter. 'She is my life, do something. You are a clever man while I am a humble salesman, jobless now', he said sobbing in despair.

Moved by Ramamoorthy's determination to save his baby, the doctor called a charitable foundation. The baby was taken in an ambulance to the Amrita Institute of Medical Sciences in Kochi, with the grandmother and father by her side. The gap in funds for the surgery was bridged by altruists.

When Rani recovered and was discharged, she instantly left for Kochi to be with her child. The surgery went well, and the baby was named Sridevi after the surgeon who operated on her.

The family are taking no chances with her health. They are grateful for the timely medical intervention and meticulously follow all the medical instructions. They regularly trek to Kochi for her post-surgery check-up.

Her third birthday was celebrated in December 2018 and it is only now that the family is less anxious about her health.

As their little girl grows, she radiates joy. The parents believe she is the Goddess Laxmi, for the father is now employed and earns about ₹3,000 a month. He is a salesman and if you find yourself in Kochi, you will recognize him instantly because of his wide grin and twinkling eyes.

Ramamoorthy believes he is twice blessed, for the birth of his daughter and her second life granted by the excellent medical team.

5
GENEROSITY ISN'T ALTRUISM

To give without any reward, or any notice,
has a special quality of its own.
—Anne Morrow Lindbergh

Effective altruism differs from other philanthropic practices because of its emphasis on quantitatively comparing charitable causes and interventions with the goal of maximizing certain moral values. Peter Singer, in his book *The Life You Can Save*, argued for the basic philosophy of effective giving, claiming that people have a moral imperative to donate more because of the existence of extreme poverty. In the book, Singer argued that people should use charity evaluators to determine how to make their donations most effective. Singer personally gives a third of his income to charity. He tries to understand what obligations do the affluent have towards those who live in extreme poverty.

There are ten common reasons why people do not give to charity. The most common is that people give to their communities and families and feel that they have given enough. Evidence from *The Selfish Gene* to social theories can explain why there is a natural desire to support local communities, but this creates a large imbalance with not enough funds being available for places and causes where the money is most needed. Ninety-five per cent of the US$240 billion that individuals in the United States give to charities annually goes to domestic non-profits while only 5 per cent is donated internationally (Singer 2009). Americans donate twice as much as individuals in other rich nations, but only a fraction goes to help people where there is the greatest need and where a dollar goes the furthest.

Even more powerful an idea from the gene-dominant theory is that money should be saved for family and the self. Sometimes it is also felt that the real problems that need to be dealt with, such as poverty alleviation or refugees in war-stricken areas, are too large for individual donations to matter. Actually, small donations can make a huge difference. The larger the problem appear to be, the greater is the chance that potential donors might feel that the problem (for instance, poverty) cannot be solved, or that it is not the real problem at all, merely a symptom of another underlying problem.

There is also widespread distrust of the aid sector, with questions often raised about the funding required to maintain bureaucracies, endemic corruption in some parts of the world and the lack of an impactful project, all of which lead to ineffectiveness of donations in solving problems. But these are merely excuses, for there are a large number of impactful social organizations that have demonstrated the effective end use deployment of funding.

Finally, there is the social belief that giving aid creates dependency and the problems are really those for governments to solve. Governments, too, would like to believe this!

There seems to be a clear gender divide in altruism as well, and this seems to be culturally specific. In the United States, the larger donations have usually come from men who seem to have greater access to income and where visible altruism is seen as a social requirement for success in careers and society. The United States also sees significant legacy giving and from retirees, who have assets beyond what they might want to pass on to family.

Comparing this across the pond with the UK, women are found to be more likely to be givers, and retirees often do not have significant assets to dispose of. However, both countries continue to have high levels of charity and giving. Also, in both countries, altruism is not merely charitable donations of money, but also volunteering and sharing expertise pro bono for the benefit of others. In the United States, volunteering is often accompanied by cash giving, while this is not so in the UK.

Continuing with the Anglo-American comparison for a moment, the United States tends to give more to causes close to home (school, college, or university they attended, the local church, the local hospital), where Britons tend to give to wider causes such as education, healthcare, the arts and environment. Americans seem to want a more direct, touchy-feely association with the causes to which they give, and give generously. International aid gets the part of British giving, followed by medical research, school and childcare, family welfare, heritage, the countryside and animal welfare. The Church of England being well-endowed requires little financial support, whereas the smaller churches in the United States often depend upon local collections for their funding.

There is much to learn from the cross-Atlantic differences in the ways of giving. Other than church collections, small donations in the United States are usually done through electronic transfers and pledges, often linked to tax savings. Small in the UK is lesser than in America and is more informal, being led by the 'collection tin' or raffles. The National Lottery has become a major mechanism for trapping self-interest with giving, becoming a major donor for charitable causes in the UK.

We could discuss other countries or go into greater depth into the two cited above, but the pattern is clear. Even between nations that are altruistic and people who are generous, there are significant differences. The giving patterns are due to a confluence of multiple factors, including the expectations of the role of government and private enterprise, the role of money and wealth in society, the structure of institutions and the organization of local communities.

Researchers have broadly identified Americans as being 'generous' while Britons are 'altruistic'. American giving is linked with self-interest (with social approval), is a more public than a private activity, and is an expression of a person's social identity and goals. Giving and volunteering are closely linked and regarded as part of civic duty. Giving and donations are well planned and intentional, and the average size is quite high. Americans also like a predominantly personal focus, looking at causes that are close to the heart of a donor. The British are generally more reserved as a people, and this is expressed in their giving also, being a more private affair. It is smaller in quantum, both individually and collectively as a nation, is less linked to personal causes and more to universal issues where there is a collective social duty to help fellow human beings.

For Americans in particular, and for much of the world, the question remains as to where should one give to have the maximum impact, both on the self and on the recipient. Donors increasingly want evidence to show that there is an impact of the work done by an organization, and perhaps by the money given by a specific donation. However, organizations and charitable institutions in the field are often not very good at providing the kind of information donors seek. The result, therefore, is that funding often reaches those organizations that have better 'customer'-relation practices than those that do not. Donors are supporting the effective altruism movement, trying to ensure that money is effectively spent and supporting those organizations that are likely to have a greater measureable impact on the ground.

A typical approach of an effective altruism network or group might seek to embark on an analysis that draws from a rich and dynamic ecosystem of not-for-profit innovation and intervention. Ultimately, this analysis will help the network (and others) determine whether they seek to 'add water to a flowing stream' (i.e., support existing initiatives, pick something from a pool of options and fund it) or work to innovate around something new. It could mean that an existing and proven model simply needs to be nuanced or configured for adjustment or transposition to new contexts.

Impact assessment is key, and the network might seek to understand the measurement of impact in broad terms and the specific range (and type) of metrics used in tracking the models that have been identified as 'best practice'. These will likely span a series of secondary and tertiary 'externalities' to any intervention. They would be interested in attempting to define immediate outputs versus longer term outcomes, and also that which is typically captured in quantitative terms versus that which must be understood in more qualitative terms. Above all, the analysis would be informed by an appreciation of the inherent complexity of these interventions, taking into account the cultural, economic/income, health and infrastructure contexts of the inputs that make a project successful, and the corresponding outputs that confirm long-term social impact, through the use and the applicability of standardized impact assessment methods.

Questions of interest include:

- How is any one of the initiatives positioned as a private intervention vis-à-vis the state?

- What are the implications of developing a wholly sustainable private effort (if it is even possible, which is not a given) when some would argue it is the duty of the state to support wholesale quality social welfare?

- What would be the relationship of these models to available public subsidies over time, if any? What would be the level of interaction between such a private model and the public system?

- Would there be some way of ensuring the flow of 'best practice' in operations across private and public silos?

- Once a particular intervention is up and running, what does its existence mean for the sector at large in a given national context? (i.e., Will there be ripple effects, distortions, catalytic changes from disruption or triggered demands from the market that were until now non-existent?)

Effective altruism networks seek to use information similar to the above to enrich their 'pipeline' of listed fundable opportunities (for both social investors and grant-makers). In recent years, the terminology itself reflects the focus: Impact Investing.

Keira: 'I believe that empathy will make the world go round. No action is too big or too small'.

Rita: 'We can't wait for someone else to act. We make the difference, our actions count, reach out and help in whatever way you can, whenever possible. That is the hope that will eventually keep societies together and us humane'.

THIS TOO SHALL PASS

No winter lasts forever; no spring skips its turn.
—Hal Borland

Jind is a city in the state of Haryana and is one of the oldest districts of the state. The fort of Jind was built by King Ganpat Singh in 1775 AD. Eleven-year-old Anish lives in a small nondescript village near Jind, with his father Rajeev and mother Neelam. He is an only child.

Anish was quite ill and as he grew older his parents were distressed to see him suffer due to his poor health. Ignorance and hope are two sides of the same coin. They explained away his condition by saying it was caused by Neelam's lack of appetite while she was pregnant. She often blamed herself for drinking too much Cola when pregnant. 'Caused gas, harmed baby in stomach', she would often tell the other women in the village.

His bouts of breathlessness, lack of appetite and chronic fatigue worried them. They overlooked it for as long as they could, but when his growth was retarded in comparison to children his age, they took him to the local doctor. The local doctor sent them onwards to the city doctor who directed them to a specialist. It was a chain; they ran from one doctor to another. Not a couple to give up easily, his parents persisted and held on to their belief in God.

'He has been suffering from a congenital heart disorder called atrial septal defect (ASD), which required a device closure, a non-invasive procedure', they were finally told.

As soon as the congenital heart disorder was detected, Rajeev took his son to different doctors and hospitals. It was a mad scramble, with the medical file getting fatter as several tests and X-rays were done.

Finally, they reached a doctor at the prestigious Max Hospital. The doctor at once saw that the family could not afford the surgery. He was, however, moved by Rajeev's love for his son. He realized that Rajeev would willingly lie down on the hospital bed in place of his son, if that would heal him. He watched as Rajeev and his wife tried everything in their control to raise the money required.

They pledged the land which until now had sustained the family. Rajeev calculated that with his monthly income of ₹7,000, it would take him more than a decade to pay back the loan that he would need to take. The problem was not with his intent but with the banks and the moneylender sharks in the village. They wanted not just the land but also eyed his wife.

The doctor stepped in quietly and, without raising Rajeev's hopes, made a few calls. A group of philanthropists stepped in and supported the family and paid for the surgery. Rajeev was overwhelmed because it was not a loan and nor was there a payback in cash or kind. They did not want his land.

Anish was taken for the device closure, and he recovered over a period of days in the hospital.

He has since rejoined school and is quite popular with his classmates despite having a speech disorder. This hasn't discouraged him from learning as much as he can. When his friends make too much noise, he cheekily points at the empty vessels suggesting that they are shallow. And then after provoking them, he runs away and hides. These are normal pranks for a special boy—a child who has not let life's setbacks stymie his enthusiasm for life.

Rajeev is relentless in his pursuit for solutions that will make his son's life easier. He regularly takes him to a local doctor in Rohtak, a fair distance from Jind. The local government has various schemes that support speech therapy and child development.

According to Rajeev, 'Anish is a happy and organized child; even though young, he is punctual and regular with his school work submitting assignments on time. He is careful about his belongings'.

Despite the hardship this young boy faces, nothing stops him from learning and keeping an open mind. He loves cycling around the neighbourhood and plays cricket with the boys in his locality.

There has been a dramatic shift in his energy level and therefore in his confidence. Before the surgery, he was lethargic and often listless. He spent most days staring at the ceiling. His growth was retarded, and he could not keep pace with other boys his age, neither physically nor academically.

A beaming Rajeev, however, says that was in the past. 'Now my son is unstoppable'. Pointing at a hoarding advertising a brand of car tyres, he says with pride, 'Unstoppable, like that'.

'We couldn't contribute anything towards the surgery and it was entirely supported by people who didn't know us', says Rajeev. 'No one in our family could come forward to help us as everyone has struggles with money'.

These days, besides school, Anish loves to watch *Motu and Patlu* on television, and eating *rasgullas* is his big treat, for which he will do anything, even extra homework!

6

WHAT MOTIVATES DONORS?

We often take for granted the very things that most deserve our gratitude.
—Cynthia Ozick

It must be reiterated that the differences between the Americans and the British in their patterns of giving are vast but are minor compared with the deeply altruistic nature of human beings as compared with other animals. That said, how we give and whom we give it to say a lot about us as individuals. Whether we give because of religious commitment, to appease a God or out of fear, family tradition or to repay a good done to us in the past or we do not give at all. In each situation, it reflects who we are and what drives us. Cultural values, individual differences and personal histories come into play, shape the emotional experience as it occurs.

There is an emotional cycle for us cognitive human beings that other animals are spared from. We respond emotionally, sinking into a downward spiral for negative emotions, or into an upward spiral for positive emotions. Positive emotions raised through positive altruistic activities can transform individuals, as we have seen from the warm glow effect, but they can also transform large groups of people and communities.

Reflecting on 'good deeds' and altruism in general can allow it to become more than a routine act and can create a spiral of positive psychology inside a person. An experiment conducted with university undergraduate students showed that they felt more deeply happy doing something philanthropic, doing something altruistic, rather than having fun. The impact on the giver of philanthropy stays for a long time, but a more superficial joy may be momentary. This is because human beings have evolved past their selfish genes to being generous, to being social, to being philanthropic. The positive feedback loop is completed as the expectation has now been built that helping other people increases well-being. Even people with depression find that they themselves are vastly helped when they find someone who needs their help.

The positive emotional impact is in detail, of course, dependent on cultural differences, gender, family structures and individual biases. The needs and concerns of donors are central to understanding why they give of themselves and their wealth.

According to the authors of *The Seven Faces of Philanthropy*, Russ Alan Prince and Karen Maru File, most donors fall into one of the seven categories or clusters that they discovered after considerable research spread over four years. Their research 'shows how different philanthropic personalities have differing levels of awareness, knowledge, and interest in the various giving strategies available to them'.

Identifying the donor-type can be valuable for a charitable organization, as it can then tailor the 'ask' more specifically to the motivations of the particular donor. But this is not an easy task, as the organization needs the tools and analytical structures to first understand the donor and then analyse what type they might best be fitted into. Donor segmentation, classification of the donors from their undifferentiated mix into a small number of groups based on similarity of views, is critical.

Statistical cluster analysis of the data set by the researchers showed the presence of four major donor segments: Affiliators, who look for social and business linkages through non-profit-related activities; Pragmatists, who seek personal financial advantages through support of non-profits; Dynasts, who are heirs to family affluence and to a tradition of philanthropy; and Repayers, who want to reciprocate benefits they or someone close to them received from a non-profit.

Within each donor segment were a myriad of factors surrounding motivation, and several identifying features, including religious alignments, gender, family traditions and the like. However, seven clear motivating ideologies were identified.

- The Communitarians: Doing Good Makes Sense
- The Devout: Doing Good Is God's Will
- The Investor: Doing Good Is Good Business
- The Socialite: Doing Good Is Fun
- The Altruist: Doing Good Feels Right
- The Repayer: Doing Good in Return
- The Dynast: Doing Good Is a Family Tradition

The largest group of donors are the Communitarians, precisely because what they do generously makes good sense! They are active in philanthropy, either in local communities or through organized not-for-profit organizations. They have an economic surplus to donate, so may be professionals or local business owners. They want to help their local community prosper, which is the modern representation of the tribal instinct. They often believe that their fortune is derived from the community, and they, in turn, want to be a part of serving the community's needs. The idea of giving back to the community may cause some superficial resemblance to the Repayers, but the Communitarians have a dominant focus on the community, which is the central reason for their giving. The Communitarians are linked deeply into their communities, have business interests there and are part of the local ecosystem. They are not uncomfortable regarding philanthropy as being a transactional exchange, where they receive the warm glow and local goodwill and recognition in return for their philanthropy. They have no issue with public acknowledgement of their good deeds. Their business, personal lives and their altruism are all part of the local community.

The Devout are the second-largest group of major donors. Their motivation is religious, and they are fulfilling God's will in helping others. Often they will quote from religious scriptures in justifying their good deeds to themselves and others. Their raison d'etre for philanthropy is their religious belief. For the Devout, those who give are more mature and spiritually developed. It is 'good to be selfless'. As this group draws their motive from scriptures, they often question the motives of others who are altruistic, implying all kinds of base motives to the rationale of others. The Devout do not care about personal recognition, as they believe that the real rewards operate on a spiritual level. Only when recognition comes within their peer group context do they find it meaningful. Additionally, as the reason is giving and not the end purpose by itself, the Devout tend not to be active in managing the spending of the funds donated. The charity is expected to be selfless and trusting, and the moral persuasion is more important than any audit of the spent funds.

The Investor category of donors sees philanthropy as good business. While they are keen on causes and monitor spending effectively, they are more concerned about the impact of giving on taxation and the breaks or refunds that they might get. They try and work with charitable organizations that are well structured to document and offer tax benefits. Investors believe that philanthropy must also be sustainable; if the giver does not get a benefit, they feel that the funding will dry up. For them, the giving is transactional. However, somewhat paradoxically, investors are sensitive to being recognized for their donations and desire both personal and public acknowledgement.

Socialites are usually extroverts, highly gregarious and linked with local networks and social groups. They believe in making the world a better place, and the fun associated with networking and giving is a reason in itself for them to be philanthropic. They enjoy participating in social events, fundraisers and donor galas. Socialites seek out their network for two reasons; first, to support their efforts, and second, as a source of validation for the causes they support. It is essential for Socialites to be individually recognized and acknowledged by the charitable organizations they support. As a consequence, working with Socialite donors is a high-maintenance activity for charitable organizations.

The altruists group are the archetypal, almost mythical, donors. They are generous and selfless, giving their time and money due to an empathy with the cause, and they very often want to remain anonymous. Altruists understand that there is inequality in the world, and they feel a moral responsibility to assist those who do not have as much as they do. Often, the giving leads to a sense of purpose of personal fulfilment for the altruist philanthropist.

Repayers, on the other hand, feel a sense of obligation because they have in the past been recipients of philanthropic assistance, and they feel the burden of having to give back. Very often, a positive change in economic and financial circumstances is immediately followed by as large a donation as the Repayer can realistically afford to make.

Dynasts usually have inherited their wealth and, probably, have a tradition of giving in their family. There is a social and family expectation that they would support charitable causes, though the type of activity supported does vary even within a family. The motivation to give is high and is internally linked to the sense of self of the family and its place in the community.

Keira: 'My mother told me, charity begins at home. And that I should have given my old clothes to my maid'.

Rita: 'Without any prejudice I can tell you that how we give and to whom we give says a lot about us as individuals. Whether we give because of religious commitment, to appease God or out of fear, family tradition or to repay a good done to us in the past. Whatever the motivation, it is a reflection of who we are.

DIVINE INTERVENTION

If you can dream it, you can do it.
—Walt Disney

Thanjavur, formerly Tanjore, is a city in the state of Tamil Nadu. Thanjavur is an important centre of South Indian religion, art and architecture.

This story is about a little girl from Thanjavur.

If you are out there, with a critically ill child, and no body to turn to, it may be amongst the worst things that can happen to you as a parent and caregiver. This is a true story, one where the human spirit to fight all odds gets the family through challenging times. This story needs a deep well of empathy and vulnerability to be able to relate to because it tells the story of a single mother trying to be everything and play every role for her children. A scenario familiar and yet often left unsung in urban India. It exposes the dark shadow over culture and society of the rich and affluent.

It is time to change the narrative; we begin with positive stories where help came from unexpected quarters. Help often, like luck, is unexpected. Life is nuanced and profound in all that it throws up.

A 13-year-old girl from the district of Thanjavur was diagnosed with a CHD within three weeks of being born. She is the youngest child born in the family. Named after the deity Durga, she exemplified courage in the face of all odds.

Durga is the youngest of five children. Her mother is the pillar of strength as their father deserted the family soon after her birth. Her mother, Karunanidhy, holds the family together. She must manage five children on her own and was then in a situation, where she was left heartbroken and clueless on how to manage a newborn who would die if she didn't get her the necessary treatment required to live. But there was nothing she could do; there were no options, so Durga went years without receiving the necessary treatment. It is difficult to put any blame on the mother. Like many people, she was suddenly exposed to a medical problem and repeated visits to the hospital clutching her ill child, something that was alien to Karunanidhy.

As a single mother, she had to work. Her salary of ₹5,000 per month was inadequate but that was all she had to look after her five children including a very ill Durga. Each time Karunanidhy took her daughter to the local doctor, she was honest and told him that she could not afford surgery, nor could she manage to raise the required amount through loans. No one was ready to lend her a rupee, so getting hundreds of thousands was out of the question.

Surgery was off the table for her, so the doctors said they would closely follow Durga's case and delay the surgery for as long as they could.

However, Durga's health deteriorated drastically as she started the third grade at school. She was unable to walk and was forced to drop out of school. She continued to stay home until 2018, and the situation was getting worse.

Karunanidhy was beside herself with worry. She felt hopeless and helpless. She watched the city around her bustle with activity, a sharp and cruel reminder of the stillness at home, of her bedridden daughter. She watched her employers spend money and cringed because she felt so poor in comparison.

As a mother, she felt broken and small. Clutching flowers on her way to work, she stopped regularly at the local temple. 'God do something', she muttered under her breath as she offered the flowers broken from the flowering bush outside the temple and made her way to work.

And, then, it seemed that the Gods smiled at her and her prayers were answered. Dr Krishna Kumar, from the Amrita Institute of Medical Sciences, Kochi, was conducting a Paediatric Cardiac Screening Camp in July 2018, where he met Durga. Her diagnosis was confirmed; she required an open-heart surgery as she was suffering with Tetralogy of Fallot. The Amrita Institute found philanthropists who decided to support Durga, thus taking the financial burden off Karunanidhy.

Karunanidhy was overjoyed. For her, Diwali had come early that year, and now she celebrates each passing day with gratitude, reminding her children that miracles do occur and that there is power in worship. She bought flowers from the local flower seller and cracked a coconut to thank God. She bought sweets and distributed them to the small children crowding the temple, for her hope had mushroomed through an undergrowth of unsurmountable problems.

Karunanidhy says, 'I am so grateful my daughter is well now; I dream that one day she will become a teacher and will spread joy. My little Durga is such a happy and active child despite facing the pain and health issues. Being the youngest of all my children and a survivor, we think she is lucky for us. Her favourite game is kho-kho, which she could not take part in for several years. She used to watch the village children play and it made me sad to see her. Now she is the local champion!'

THE ULTIMATE AIM OF ALTRUISM

*Hope begins in the dark,
the stubborn hope that if you just
show up and try to do the right thing,
the dawn will come.*
—Anne Lamott

So, let us now move away from the donors to focus a little bit on the recipients of philanthropy. Altruism tends to improve health and well-being; it generally improves happiness, while not always making everyone happy.

But why should we bother to improve happiness? The strongest motivation, perhaps, is that the world is an increasingly dangerous place, and the lives of so many people are truly unhappy. There has been a remarkable increase in depression in the last 50 years. And it is affecting people at younger and younger ages. Clinically depressed teenagers are no longer a rarity. The depression and unhappiness may come from external sources, of war and natural disasters, or depression may be due to unhappiness that is not related to sustenance and survival.

If you do not have it, then money and the material possessions it can buy are quite important. However, money and material possessions are not as important to happiness as we often think. Policy-makers tend to focus on increasing our spending power, on the assumption that with more in our pockets and a wider range of choices to spend it on, we will feel happy and prosperous. Prosperity is important to us, but once we have enough money to cater for our basic needs, money is not on its own enough to create a sense of well-being in individuals or societies.

The world has seen a decade and more of people from relatively affluent societies fomenting violence on others, dispossessing many, and also the counter-revolution of public movements in countries that are not exactly starving. What then is the role of altruism and philanthropy? Is it only to help those who are completely helpless, or may it also try and create a better world for us all? If we want to reduce the high levels of ill health, crime and poverty that plague many of our communities and if we want to see our children blossom and develop into fully rounded adults, then spreading a little more happiness is a surprisingly effective and inexpensive way of achieving our goal.

Achieving happiness in our societies has to be one of the ultimate aims of altruism. The problems of the world need new solutions, and happy people are more persistent in attempting to solve problems. They give in less often; they work away at complicated tasks for longer than people who are unhappy. Happy people are, in general, more altruistic than unhappy people too. They have more empathy with those in need and are more generous when it comes to donating time and money to charities. Happy people are less focused on themselves; they are keen to share their good fortune with others.

They have more persistence, they are better at problem-solving and exploration, they are more independent than their peers, and they approach life with more enthusiasm. Happy children find it easier to build relationships and friendships; they have more casual friends and more close friends than their less happy peers.

Happiness is also worth bothering about because happy people are healthier people. Studies into the elderly found that those who were happy, optimistic or generally satisfied with life had much less risk of dying than those who were unhappy or pessimistic. Other research has found that people who are happy and contented seem to be at less risk from conditions like hypertension, heart disease, diabetes, colds and upper respiratory infections. When they receive a flu vaccine, people who are rated as very happy by psychologists develop more antibodies than the average person does. The other side of the coin is that depression can exacerbate the impact of a wide range of illnesses.

And happy people cope better with illness. It does not matter what your economic condition is. If you have hope and happiness about your future, you are able to deal with ill health better than those who feel they have no hope. A positive outlook seems to reduce the perception of pain amongst people who are ill.

Happy people live longer—it is true! A study of 180 nuns demonstrated that those who started out in their vocation with an optimistic outlook generally lived longer than their more pessimistic sisters did. A large-scale research project which tracked the lives of more than 2,000 Mexicans, aged over 65 and living and working in the United States, found that those who had a positive outlook on life were half as likely to die and half as likely to become disabled.

And, finally, the economic powerhouse of the world needs happy workers, who it turns out are productive workers. Since 1998, pollsters at Gallup have surveyed the happiness levels of the US workforce. In September 2004, about a quarter of workers said that they felt engaged with their work, with over half being not engaged. In analysing their research, Gallup argues that many employers fail to understand that while pay and benefits are important to their staff, they are not the clinching factors in whether people are happy at work. What people want is a supportive boss and strong friendships amongst their colleagues.

In general, happy people are much more positive about life. A positive frame of mind makes us much more creative, generous and constructive. We seek what is right in a topic, not what is wrong. Thinking out of the box is much easier when we are positive because we see more opportunities and potential. When we feel negative, we search for problems, reasons for not doing things, for not hiring a particular individual, for not pursuing up a new opportunity.

While some not-for-profit organizations focus on how bad everything is, and how unhappy all the people are, this does not, fortunately, extend to all the charitable organizations. Most want to propagate success stories of rising out from troubles to becoming self-sufficient.

But negative stories and milking them for funding is what is prevalent in mass media. A lot of this has to do with journalism and with what pays off in journalism. The good life, the positive, is not just the absence of the negative. Why are there so few stories about a positive human future? Positive psychology has a lot to offer to journalism. First of all, it's important to think about what are your ethical values when you report on the world. Are you only here to point out what is wrong, and what's dissent, and where politicians disagree? Or, should journalism also be looking at where you can collaborate, where politicians have visions for communities and the citizens that they serve?

Many people have an overly negative view of the world. Victimhood is central to the thesis. We assume that people are victims of hardship. We assume that politicians have to fight and disagree. We assume that if a natural disaster happens, it is all about misery and losing lives and setbacks. But in the same scenario, you will find people who collaborate, people who help each other and people who grow from trauma. The research findings from positive psychology offer a bigger outlook on the world, which makes us portray the world more accurately.

Negative news sells media space, but it has a deep impact on society. Stories of altruism that made a difference need to get out there, to be uplifting and positive and offering an alternative vision of the world.

Attitude is everything. There are two sides to every story. To give up or thrive is a choice; Sheela and Ravi[14] would have been reduced to victims, but they scripted a different story for their own lives.

Strangely enough, even though many people think from the news that the world is worse, by every statistic known, the world is a better place than ever before. But the question is, given that the world is better, why do people think the world is worse?

The Economist is a good example of positive psychology while reporting stories. The *BBC World Service* is doing a lot on this, and it is because it wants to portray the world more accurately. *The Guardian*, the British newspaper, is doing this across many of its products. The Dutch media, online media called *De Correspondent*, is doing this progressively and boldly. They are actually going into being activists about some issues, creating events in real life to enable people make other choices. So, they are actually also taking on the role of facilitating societal change in real life.

Playing an activist role is controversial in journalism, and this trend has been seen in television news channels in India recently. The conventional view is that journalists need to be detached, they need to mirror the world, not make the world. However, that has always been a myth, the journalist as a dispassionate observer. Journalism influences thinking and decision-making. So, it is moving the world by influencing the way people think and then affecting the decisions by creating a polarization in society.

It is important to understand this bigger worldview. Journalists know a lot about negative emotions, about positive traumatic stress, about victims. They have seen a lot. It is a form of learned helplessness. Journalists know a lot about negative relationships, dissent and conflicts, and disagreement. But do they know enough about the positives?

---

[14] The children from the chapter Beginnings.

There is an alternative narrative of learned optimism, resilience, grit, the concept of post-traumatic growth and the broaden-and-build principle: that positive emotions really expand your outlook and foster creativity and collaboration. Interviews and stories can be presented from positive emotions rather than always drawing out what hurts and what is not working.

Society, and the news media, needs to reflect, expand their thinking, so that the public understanding of major issues is dealt with in a critical and reflective manner, rather than in a critical and negative manner.

Constructive journalistic stories are meaningful and uplifting, but they have high societal significance, and they adhere to core functions in journalism, like being a watchdog and giving the public important information about society. Those are the definitions that we currently work with and would make us able to measure what are positive journalistic stories and what are constructive journalistic stories. Constructive journalism is a growing domain. There is a lot of experimentation going on, and depending on which newspaper or newsroom you ask, they tend to do different experimentation.

There are signs of a different kind of journalism. First, there are many more solutions-oriented stories in the news. If the news points out a problem, they are also trying to cover a potential solution, or point to a solution, or look for a solution.

Another constructive element in journalism is facilitating a future-oriented debate, instead of always looking back and being critical with perfect hindsight. Are there visionary public news debates that you can remember, perhaps including politicians or decision makers that you can remember that made a real difference to society? Have stories played out in the news media that focus on a better tomorrow? Where are we headed as a society? How can we get there? What will you do to get us there? How will you collaborate with your opponent or your party members to get us there? A simple test is to look at any election cycle. The questions that journalists put to politicians usually focus on the past, while when voters get to ask questions to politicians, the majority of the questions are oriented towards the future. Voters, citizens, are interested in where we are headed.

A constructive element in journalism could, therefore, add and facilitate a future orientation and facilitate a visionary future-oriented debate. And a powerful way to do this is to look at the work done by altruistic and charitable organizations, where they have brought smiles to the faces of people who have very little.

Keira: 'I don't watch prime time TV. It is so negative; one would believe that nothing is right with the world'.

Rita: 'Bad news makes news. Good news is boring and doesn't get TRPs. But we can make our own news and share positivity'.

Keira: 'Rita, knowing you, newspaper barons and media heads had better watch out. We will spread good news and stories that uplift, stories about ordinary people doing extraordinary things'.

Rita: 'And you can start by doing something that adds happiness to someone's day. Why don't you volunteer at that orphanage that you mentioned the other day?'

Keira: 'Will that help me feel better about the break up with my boyfriend or forget the boss's comments?'

Rita: 'Try it; spread some cheer and it may move the clouds that seem to darken your mood. You can't fool me, I have seen through your forced gaiety and looked beyond your Instagram profile'.

WHEN PRAYERS ARE ANSWERED

Believe you can, and you are half way there.
—Theodore Roosevelt

The birth of a child is special, and each new life must be celebrated. However, an ill child's suffering is very difficult to watch. It can break even the toughest person. It is tempting to romanticize these situations especially if the outcome is positive. However, it is important to remember that the situation is even more heart-wrenching if the parents are poor, marginalized and struggle to eke out a living by performing backbreaking work for survival.

Five-day-old Manisha was the second child born to Archana and Onbir, who live in Haryana.

Onbir is a farmer who earns ₹3,500 a month. To supplement his income, he often takes visitors to the major tourist attraction of the area, the Rani Talaab. Uneducated though he was, he had learnt the history of the place by rote and would, for a paltry sum, entertain tourists to augment his income. He is the bread earner for his small family, and it is his earnings that support his wife and two children. Because of innovation in agricultural methods and the induction of technology, his agricultural labour is low paying and he is losing out on progress of the economy. The dichotomy between change and tradition is clear. He is aware that his father would have scoffed at his feeble attempt to be tour guide, but this is a new world and he has adapted to it.

His second child, Manisha, was a daughter, and he was happy that both mother and child were well. Their happiness was short-lived. Immediately after her birth, both parents were shocked when the doctors told them that their baby had turned blue and was showing worrying signs and had difficulty in breathing.

The new mother, Archana, ached to see her daughter. However, the newborn was immediately after birth taken away to be stabilized before being rushed to Jaypee Hospital in Noida. The infant had to make her first foray into the world via an ambulance ride, a journey of 200 km soon after birth, leaving her worried mother in the hospital to recover after the delivery.

As soon as she arrived at the hospital, an echocardiogram test was conducted. The diagnosis was severe. It showed that she was suffering from a CHD called transposition of great arteries (TGA) and there were four leaflets in Manisha's aortic valve, when in normal cases there are only three.

This made the case extremely unique. Manisha required an arterial switch operation. Onbir was unable to grasp the big words, but what he did get through to him was the urgency of the situation and the grave danger to his child if she did not get medical help in time.

There was really no hope. No hope and no future for his daughter. He was crushed; his situation weighed him down. For the first time, he questioned his own existence and the meaning of life. 'Why me? Why my daughter? And if it had to be my child then why make me so poor?' he questioned God in his mind. The unfairness of it all made him angry.

He paced the corridor nervously almost colliding into a lady doctor. One look at him and she knew that he was on the verge of a breakdown. She calmly heard his story and assured him that she would try her best.

He had little faith in her words.

And yet, good things do happen. She contacted an altruistic foundation, and Onbir was told that the financial requirement had been met.

Just like that, in a minute, his life looked up. It was as if the sun had come out from behind dense clouds and the dark shadow was cast behind him.

Since the surgery, Manisha has shown great change. She is a happy child and loves to play with her mother and sister. Onbir now has a new job in a private company as he aspires to do better and wants to give his daughters the best. He wants them to be better than he is, to reach for the skies and pull out a few stars because he believes that prayers get answered, even impossible ones. He says, 'My daughter was granted a new life. I really hope that one day she achieves her dream of becoming a doctor—a heart specialist—so we as a family are able to help other children'.

8

TRANSFORMING LIVES CAN LEAD TO HAPPINESS

> *What we constantly aspire to be,*
> *that in some sense we are.*
> —Anna Jameson

Happiness is sometimes associated with managing expectations. Are you happy with less only because you began with less? This is another central question in looking at altruism.

An indicator comes from evidence that it is the change in a person's circumstance rather than the absolute position of success of the person that defines happiness. Self-improvement and success often occur together. But that does not necessarily mean they are the same thing. Our culture today is obsessively focused on unrealistically positive expectations: Be happier. Be healthier. Be the best, better than the rest. Be smarter, faster, richer, more popular and more admired. With this imagery comes low self-worth, as most of us are not able to meet our own expectations, because they march ahead just as we are reaching them.

Conventional self-help aims to discover a person's limitations and work at the edges. We are focussing on what we do not have. It is like the Mist of Ignorance, with human beings wandering through the clouds, parting the mist to discover something else they lack. The obsession with progress has a fundamental assumption ... that you have space to progress, and therefore are in an unhappy place at the present.

Charities working with people at the edges of society do not have the luxury of offering progress as a hope. Sometimes people have to accept and live out the lives they have. And the smiles in these most depressing of situations show that happiness and fulfilment need not have a progress-focus all the time.

If you focus on your shortcomings and failures, then figure out ways to progress, you will always be unhappy. You will never reach the goal ... the state of happiness. The desire for more positive experience is itself a negative experience. And, paradoxically, the acceptance of one's negative experience is itself a positive experience.

At its core, the acceptance of what is, rather than changing it, is core to Buddhist and similar philosophies. Living in the present, accepting it, realizing that problems are often here to stay, by itself brings solutions. Problems sometimes do not go away, they just become better.

The other reality is that problems are rarely unique. If there is a problem, the chance is high that a lot of other people have had similar problems in the past, have them at present and are likely to have them in the future. The problem does not become any less for an individual if others have it too, no. What it means is that the problem is not unique to the individual and the person is not always a victim. This does not take away the severity of the problem but is often the first step in finding a solution to it.

Charitable social organizations usually work with people who have deep problems. Making the person realize that they are not alone sometimes leads to a way out. If not, then perhaps a better acceptance of reality, and therefore the space to find some happiness.

Many religious and philosophical traditions have taught us to accept what happens in one's life, some calling it destiny or 'karma', while others attributing the morality of our actions and deeds on what comes to pass. The extreme and usually incorrect interpretation of such externalization leads to despair, as there is no path seen to get oneself out of a difficult or unhappy situation. However, a clearer understanding of the traditions says nothing of the sort; there is always a way to better your circumstances, no matter how horrible they might be. This is the space where altruism plays the greatest role, in giving hope and courage to those who have very little, along with practical ways to move forward.

Amongst the various traditions that lead from acceptance to hope, we will pick only two; and this is not to say that other traditions are not equally powerful in dealing with despair and transforming it to hope.

The Buddhist traditions emerged from the teachings of the Buddha, who argued that an acceptance of the reality of pain and suffering is the only way to move ahead in your life and attain freedom from want, pain and suffering. At the core of Buddhist teachings are the Four Noble Truths. The First Noble Truth is that life is suffering. To live, you must suffer. It is impossible to live without experiencing some kind of suffering. We have to endure physical suffering such as sickness, injury, tiredness, old age and eventually death, and we have to endure psychological suffering such as loneliness, frustrations, fear, embarrassment, disappointment, anger and so on. This is not a road to despair though; it is merely a statement of an experience, a truth, and a reality that everyone experiences and that everyone is trying to overcome. It makes no predictions on what will happen next, and neither does it deny that happiness exists. It goes right into the core of every individual human being's concern—suffering and how to avoid it.

The Second Noble Truth is that all suffering is caused by craving. It might seem odd to speak of cravings when the completely dispossessed have nothing, but craving is not to be confused with greed. When we want something, whether out of need or greed, but are unable to get it, we feel frustrated. When we expect someone to live up to our expectation and they do not, we feel let down and disappointed. When we want others to like us and they do not, we feel hurt. Even when we want something and are able to get it, this does not often lead to happiness either because it is not long before we feel bored with that thing, lose interest in it and start to want something else. The Second Noble Truth clarifies that merely getting what you think you want does not guarantee happiness. Buddhist teachings tell us to modify our behaviour; rather than linking happiness with achieving what we want, we should modify the want itself. There is a distinction between what we need and what we want, and we must strive for our needs and modify our wants. Our needs can be fulfilled, but our wants are endless, a bottomless pit. There are needs that are essential, fundamental and that can be obtained, and this we should work towards. Desires beyond this should be gradually lessened.

The Third Noble Truth is that suffering can be overcome and happiness attained. This is perhaps the most important of the Four Noble Truths because it reassures that true happiness and contentment are possible. When we give up craving and learn to live each day at a time, enjoying without continual wanting, enduring the problems that life throws at us, then we become happy and free. Because we are no longer obsessed with satisfying our own selfish wants, we find we have so much time to help others fulfil their needs. The ultimate state of achieving pure freedom from want leads to Nirvana.

The Fourth Noble Truth gives the path leading to the overcoming of suffering. This path is called the Noble Eightfold Path and consists of Perfect Understanding, Perfect Thought, Perfect Speech, Perfect Action, Perfect Livelihood, Perfect Effort,

Perfect Mindfulness and Perfect Concentration. The steps on the Noble Eightfold Path cover every aspect of life: the intellectual, the ethical, the social and economic and the psychological.

From the other side of the world comes another tradition that is centred on acceptance leading to happiness. It helps avoid self-paralysis, which can lead to self-destruction, and allows for positive action that helps lead to potentially improving your situation. This is the Ancient Greek tradition of Stoicism.

Around 300 BC in Athens, Zeno of Citium taught through lectures given while walking around a painted porch, a 'stoa poikile'. That later led to the term 'Stoicism'. Stoicism teaches the development of self-control and fortitude as a means of overcoming destructive emotions. It does not seek to remove emotions completely, but rather seeks to transform them to enable a person to develop clear judgement, inner calm and freedom from suffering (which, like Buddhism, is considered the ultimate goal).

As a philosophy, the goal of Stoicism is freedom from anguish or suffering,[15] through the pursuit of reason and apathy.[16] It teaches indifference and develops the ability to have a passive reaction to external events and equanimity in the face of life's highs and lows. The practice of Stoicism involves developing four cardinal virtues:[17] wisdom, courage, justice and temperance. There is an element of Determinism in the philosophy, which essentially recognizes that people will normally do as the necessity of the world compels us. However, Stoicism assures us that we follow the world in a conscious and deliberate manner, as only a rational being can, giving our assent to actions and events that happen to us.

Over time, Stoicism became the foremost and most influential school of philosophy of the Greco-Roman world. The most

---
[15] Which the ancients called 'passion'.
[16] In its ancient sense of being objective, unemotional and having clear judgement.
[17] Taken from the teachings of Plato.

important practical application was training oneself to separate what you can control from what you cannot control, and then focussing on what you can control. This idea of the dual 'Locus of Control' and 'Locus of Influence' has been taken up by modern business coaches and philanthropic workers as a means to emotional reactivity and enable positive action. Stoicism, therefore and like Buddhism, is not just a set of beliefs or ethical claims, but rather a way of life, involving constant practice and training. It includes the practice of logic, Socratic dialogue, self-reflection and mindfulness, the ability to remain in the present moment.[18]

Seneca the Younger, of one the famous Stoic philosophers and writers, said: 'We suffer more often in imagination than in reality'. He suggested a practical way to deal with this issue, by looking at the 'pre-meditation of evils'. This involves visualizing the worst-case scenarios that you fear, in detail, that are preventing you from taking action, so that you can take action to overcome that paralysis. Both for the altruist and the recipient of the assistance, moving away from paralysis of thought and action into positive activity is important. The first step is in recognizing the fears, of the worst that might happen. This is whatever you fear, whatever is causing you anxiety, whatever you are putting off. It involves facing up to the issue that concerns you, be it escape from a war zone, or facing a life-threatening illness or just not having enough food to eat. It could be anything. For the social worker, it could be the fear of not having the resources to deal with the situation at hand or being swamped by the extent of what needs to be done. The first step imagines all the worst things that might come to pass. Then come the next steps, dealing with what might come to pass, and reimagining a better future.

This idea has been taken forward in the modern era by thinkers such as Dan Gilbert, who says: 'Easy choices, hard life. Hard

---

[18] The term 'stoic' in modern usage has come to commonly refer to someone who is unemotional or indifferent to pain, pleasure, grief or joy. This is not the philosophical meaning and we are using the term 'stoic' in its original sense.

choices, easy life'. People make bad decisions due to errors in estimating the odds they are going to succeed. People make bad decisions due to errors in estimating the values of their own success.

In making choices about their lives, especially those who have been displaced from formerly better lives, there is a tendency to compare with the past. This causes people to pass up what is a good situation and the better cause of action, in anticipation that something even better will come along. With time, when the 'good deal' is no longer available, people in stress situation will take up an 'awful deal' because it is the only deal available. Thus, hanging on to the past can cause a person to pass up the better alternative and have to settle for suboptimal outcomes.

Human beings are particularly bad at decision-making in the sense of how nature designed us, for we have no significant predators other than ourselves, we have controlled our physical environment even if we have not necessarily improved it, and we seem to be the only species on the planet that controls its own fate. The sum of our fears is in us, the only thing that seems to be able to destroy us are our own decisions. If we underestimate the needs of the planet and focus only on a human development approach, we might have stepped into a world that no longer sees us around 10,000 years from now, or very much sooner.

So many of the problems faced by the world are of our own creation. Natural disasters are exacerbated by overdevelopment and deforestation, leading to situations where philanthropy needs to step in and ameliorate the disastrous effects of exploitation of the planet. And not always the ones who exploited natural resources are the ones who have to bear the brunt of the consequences. Many other situations, from war and genocide, to overpopulation and disease are also the consequence of human decisions. It is in this space that altruism steps in.

But there are some areas, such as health, ageing and life-threatening diseases, that are not in a significant way the result of human decisions. They exist and are just so. Cancer and heart disease may kill you and may never have been the result of human action. The most vulnerable are always the youngest and the most elderly amongst us.

The debate amongst philanthropists has a sharp divide. There are those who argue that most effort should be directed towards the systemic and long-term benefits to people, to improve healthcare, sanitation and food habits from an early age, so that the benefits of a higher life expectancy can accrue to many. There are others who argue that the immediate problem is acute and that one cannot abandon those critically ill in order to focus on general health improvement. From a donor's perspective, it is often difficult to be farsighted and seek future gains, and there are many who would rather direct their energies and money in to positively impact the lives of those most affected at that moment. One of the problems with making decisions about the far future and the near future is that we can imagine the near future much more vividly than we can the far future. However, once the level of detail of analysis can be increased in both the immediate and the far future, sensible decision-making on the allocation of resources can be done. There will also be some specialization amongst aid givers; some would like to help people suffering today, while others might want to take a systemic approach. The normal human tendency is to look at the immediate, what you can see right now. Which is why it is easier to raise money to help the victims of a landslide after the event, rather than to raise money in advance to carry out reforestation and hillside repair work in advance. It is easier to get support for care homes for those abused, than to fund an extended campaign to end the abuse in society.

If the aim of philanthropy and charity is to move more and more people to live sustainable, secure and fulfilling lives, then an understanding of the factors that lead to a well-lived and fulfilling life is needed. This is the study of 'Positive Psychology', or colloquially, the scientific study of what makes life most worth living. Similar to our journey to discover the genesis of altruism, positive psychology works at different levels, encompassing the biological, cultural, psychological, personal and relational aspects of life. It looks at eudaimonia, or 'the good life', and reflects on the factors that contribute the most to a fulfilling life. Also linked to our understanding of altruism is the role of 'happiness' and what it really means in psychological terms.

Professor Martin Seligman is the Zellerbach Family Professor of Psychology in the University of Pennsylvania's Department of Psychology. Widely regarded as the founder of Positive Psychology, his ideas about 'learned helplessness' are extremely helpful in our understanding of the motivations of altruism and the behaviour of people involved. Professor Seligman argues that psychology must have a mission that goes beyond curing the mentally ill, in addition to its mission of making miserable people less miserable. Can psychology help, he asks, in actually making people happier? An answer to this question would provide valuable tools to altruists who seek to make people happy, along with helping people recognize that desire and want lead to unhappiness.

Seligman identifies three types of happiness and believes that they are quite distinct from each other. It is possible to have one rather than the other. The first happy life is the pleasant life. This is a life in which you have as much positive emotion as you possibly can, and the skills to amplify it. The second is a life of engagement: a life in your work, your parenting, your love, your leisure; time stops for you. And the third is a meaningful life.

The research results surprised the American psychologists, but readers of this book would not be so surprised. It turns out that the pursuit of pleasure has almost no contribution to life satisfaction. The pursuit of meaning is the strongest factor. The pursuit of engagement is also very strong. Pleasure comes in if you have both engagement and meaning; then pleasure is the additional. A full life contains all three types of happiness, which add up in a manner where the sum is greater than the parts. However, if you have none of the three, defined as the empty life, then the sum is less than the parts.

The practice of psychiatry and the study of psychology, particularly in the United States since the Second World War, have had a tremendous impact in reducing depression and in providing the tools to ameliorate feelings of misery. Mental ill health is regarded as a disease, and there have been great advances in the science of dealing with mental health issues and 'curing' them. There were three consequences of this success though. By pushing the disease model, psychologists created patients and victims who needed to be treated, and the cause of the misery was external to the person. The individual need not feel any moral responsibility for the mental health issues. Personal choices and decision-making were ignored. The second consequence was that psychology became concerned only with those who were 'ill', and it forgot about improving the lives of those who were not patients of mental health 'diseases'. The mission of altruism, to improve and make people happier, whether they were in serious trouble or were leading normal lives, was in direct conflict with the aims of psychology. There was little work done on making the lives of people more fulfilled and more productive. And the third related consequence was that with the dominance of the disease model and attempts to find psycho-medical cures for patients, positive interventions for individuals or groups of people were ignored.

That was what led Seligman, Dan Gilbert and others to work on what they called 'positive psychology'. Psychology should be just as concerned with human strength as it was with weakness, with building strength as with repairing damage. It should be interested in the best things in life. And it should be just as concerned with making the lives of normal people fulfilling.

As the work developed, researchers found that they could measure different forms of happiness. Could an individual's state of positive emotion be measured against thousands of other people? This would be powerful for interventions and for the ways in which modern philanthropy was evolving, for it could be used for measurement and evaluation of programmes, if it was accepted that happiness was one measure of success.

To create such a measure, the psychologists had to move away from the diagnostic and prescriptive algorithms that existed and create a classification of strengths and virtues. Attributes were factored using discriminators such as the sex ratio, cultural parameters and ethnic experiences. The team found that they could discover the causation of the positive states, the relationship between left hemispheric activity and right hemispheric activity, as a cause of happiness.

This completed the loop and interconnection of positive psychology and altruism. There were alternative paths to happiness. The first path, positive emotion; the second path is *eudaimonian* flow; and the third path is meaning. And meaning, in this context, referred to knowing one's strengths even in situations of adversity and using them to belong to and in the service of something larger than you are. This was the very effort that altruists had always aimed for, to have people whom they were helping assist them in helping themselves and others around them. With positive psychology, additional tools became available.

With the additional tools of positive psychology at our disposal, let us look again at human beings as altruists. How do people who are recipients of aid differ from their situation just prior to that, when they were in great need? They do not differ on the basis of gender or religion or any such superficial characteristic. The only great difference is that they have moved from isolation in an extremely social context. They are no longer alone; they are each in some relationship with others.

Psychologists have carried out controlled experiments with random-assignment, placebo-controlled, long-term studies of different interventions to understand what are the things that have lasting impact on improving the lives of people. And improving lives not in a material sense or a security sense, though those practical parameters are no doubt important; the improvement of lives is in a meaningful way. How can we create the kinds of interventions that will have an effect: teach people about the pleasant life, how to have more pleasure in your life, have a meaningful life once again?

Ultimately, the net goal of charity, philanthropy and altruism is to enhance the life satisfaction of people. That is really what it is all about. So, psychologists created a measure of life satisfaction and made it their target variable in a series of studies with thousands of people. To what extent do the pursuit of pleasure, the pursuit of positive emotion, the pleasant life, the pursuit of engagement, time stopping for you and the pursuit of meaning contribute to life satisfaction?

It turns out that the skills of happiness, the skills of the pleasant life, the skills of engagement and the skills of meaning are different from the skills of relieving misery. An interesting mechanism has been found in the use of information, design, communication, entertainment and technology. These have been found to increase happiness, to increase positive emotion. But they can be used to increase meaningful engagement with life as well, and this is a learning that people working in distressed and conflict areas might well use.

As has been said: 'The time is now, the place is here, we are the people'. With the development of interesting technology, entertainment and design, we have the instruments to transform lives with meaning.

Keira: 'I just bought a Gucci bag. I have wanted that for a long time but why doesn't it make me happy?'

Rita: 'The answer', as Bob Dylan puts it, 'is blowing in the wind. More and more consumption doesn't necessarily add up to greater happiness'.

A SHOT AT NORMAL LIFE

Being deeply loved by someone gives you strength, while loving someone deeply gives you courage.
—Lau Tzu

Varanasi, also known as Benares or Kashi, is a city on the banks of the river Ganga in the state of Uttar Pradesh in North India, 320 kilometres south-east of Lucknow, the state capital. It is a major religious hub and considered sacred.

In a small colony not far from the ghats, there lived a little girl called Priya with her mother Roopam. Roopam works for a family and performs domestic chores for them. She supports her little daughter and her elderly father, who they stay with.

A CHD called Tetralogy of Fallot is enough to baffle the strongest person. It sounds every bit as formidable as it really is. And when it is about a little girl and her single mother, it assumes shades of black in terms of complexity. Add to this that the mother is illiterate and earns less than ₹3,000 a month and the situation veers on to hopelessness. The plot seems to have run away with life.

Priya was four years old when she was diagnosed with this condition. Her mother clearly remembers that fateful day; it was a sunless morning and the news inked her world black.

Life throws challenges, and the human spirit catches them and tosses them back. Roopam, when faced with the daunting task of looking after a very sick child, decided that she wasn't going to give in or give up on her daughter, although she did have her weak moments.

The travel from Varanasi to Delhi with a small baby and almost no savings was itself a herculean task for the young mother. Had it not been for the support of her father, she would not have been able to take this bold step. Society was cruel, often taunting her for being foolish. Her neighbours felt that it was wasteful expenditure to even dream of surgery, after all the child was a girl. Sick and girl being the operative words, that made them lose interest and move on.

It is not easy to live under social scrutiny. There were times that Roopam felt so hopeless that she wanted to kill herself, but persisted because Priya was a sweet-tempered child. 'It isn't her fault; every child has the right to live', she would reason with herself wearily as she stared into the darkness. Her father would look into her eyes and assure her that the breaking dawn would bring answers.

And it did. Almost magically, philanthropists stepped in and Priya got the treatment she needed.

Her first surgery took place when Priya was barely six months old. It was a BT shunt and was done at the Max Hospital in Delhi. Her second surgery took place at the age of four—which was a complete correction, and fortunately her pulmonary valve had been preserved, which means that no more interventions are required and she can live a close to normal life.

Little Priya has big dreams; she wants to be an actress. She loves to sing and recite poems, and her face lights up when she tells stories! Not one to lag on the play field, she takes part actively in all sports that are played in school. Her favourite, of course, is to jump over puddles with her friends when it rains.

After a tough day, it is a hug from Priya that lifts Roopam's spirits. She listens quietly as her daughter narrates what happened in school, pulling out a pencil and her notebook.

After dinner, Priya teaches her mother what she has learnt that day. Roopam can now sign her name and understands phrases in English. She aspires to join a shop as a retail attendant. Her daughter wants more from life and in her small way is encouraging her mother to expand her world, much to the absolute delight of her grandfather.

Priya is in school and has many friends. She continues to sing and dance and is a good mimic. She can pretend to be any actress and is so good that always gets the main lead in the school's annual day. She loves watching Hindi movies with her friends.

9

LOVE IS A TWO-WAY STREET

Don't be yourself—Be someone a little nicer.
—Mignon McLaughlin

The popular culture trend suggests that sensational stories get more public attention, and we, too, are partially to be held responsible for this as we undervalue honest, positive and unembellished stories. We tend to follow the same principle in our lives. Positive emotions have received little attention in the past. It has seemed to be more important to look for what ails the world, for the good can take care of itself. There is a tendency to focus on what is going wrong, what afflicts humanity, what are the evil vices out there and who is oppressing whom. Positive emotions are perhaps more difficult to study, for the feelings of happiness and the expressions of them are difficult to distinguish from each other. However, the three major negative emotions of fear, anger and sadness are easier to differentiate.

Evidence was found when three psychologists at the University of Kentucky—Deborah Danner, David Snowdon and Wallace Friesen—were conducting a large study on ageing and Alzheimer's disease. They came across short, personal essays written by young Catholic nuns in the 1930s, about their lives. The essays covered the spectrum of their lives, from semi-religious events in their childhood, to formal school and the religious experiences that eventually moved them to becoming nuns. The purpose of the essays was to direct the future career path of the nuns in the Roman Catholic Church. When the Kentucky researchers studied the essays, they chose to score them while looking for positive emotional content. They read the biographical sketches, looking for and recording instances of happiness, interest, love and hope. What they found astounded them. A highly positive correlation was found between the positive emotions expressed by the nuns and their life expectancy, with the nuns who expressed the most positive emotions living up to 10 years longer than those who expressed the fewest.[19]

Several other studies confirmed the hypothesis that positive emotions and longevity were highly correlated. Factoring out for other effects, a tentative suggestion of causality was also made. But with this came the question whether there were other benefits that could result from experiencing positive emotions?[20] Additionally, could positive emotions counteract and undo the harmful effects of negative emotions on individuals and on society? And we, of course, are interested in this relationship because the outcomes we are looking for may well be dependent upon how we handle positive and negative emotions in the people we extend our help to.

Negative emotions could be studied physiologically, as they had clearly understood effects on the human body, including cardiovascular activity, which could be measured. It was reasoned that the body's response to negative emotions was to get charged up for immediate and specific action. Stress, a related symptom due to negative emotions, could also lead to heart diseases and brain strokes if continued for extended periods of time.

---

[19] It should be noted that correlations must not be confused with causality. Evidence such as this cannot be used to draw cause–effect inferences.
[20] Other than the obvious feel good!

There is an added complication. We are sometimes hesitant in clearly expressing the trauma or disconnect or anguish felt by people in our world of altruism, by people we help. We use euphemisms, we hedge our words so that people are not traumatized further by our language itself. Often the people seeking assistance have lost touch with a normal world and are in an extremely disordered state. Euphemisms about their state make it appear as if their reality may not quite be as bad as it seems, or that their perception of reality might itself be flawed. Our use of the language adds a further burden to those who need our help.

It is the mind-set that has to change, to change from being passive recipients of aid to becoming active participants in their own future. Optimism, resilience and goal pursuit are all related constructs. The mind-set has to be ready to overcome obstacles, plan around them and persevere in the face of obstacles.

Altruism is not merely about being a donor, about giving out aid or lavishing money on those who have less than you do. Just as it is necessary to make the recipient rooted in their reality, and work positively towards happiness, it is also important for the altruist to be sensitive to the emotions and body language of those they are trying to help. Material needs may be satisfied by donations, but true healing requires an emotional connect.

In working with people who need help, it is important to have or develop emotional intelligence.[21] Not only do altruists need to understand the context of the problem they are trying to solve, but they also need to be aware with people, in whatever setting they find themselves, of what is happening in the emotional life. If they can sense these emotions and, likewise, express emotions appropriately, there will be a connect between the giver and the receiver that goes beyond the material and a deeper understanding of the needs that go with the problems. This is difficult even when we are aware of what emotion we want to express, because the relationship between a giver and a receiver is unbalanced.

---

[21] The term is drawn from Daniel Goleman's book by the same name.

Emotional intelligence is important in the field for another reason; it helps discriminate between accurate, honest and inaccurate or dishonest feelings.

Emotions will be both pleasant ones and unpleasant ones. We need to understand our emotions and those of others, and channel these emotions to achieve positive outcomes. This ability, extending Howard Gardner's multiple intelligences, has come to be known as emotional intelligence.[22]

The Mayer–Salovey model of emotional intelligence[23] comprises four branches of abilities we have in our emotional life, and these have functional relevance to the practice of altruism and effective philanthropy:

- The ability to perceive emotions in oneself and others accurately.

- The ability to use emotions to facilitate thinking.

- The ability to understand emotions, emotional language and the signals conveyed by emotions.

- The ability to manage emotions so as to attain specific goals.

American author Ursula LeGuin draws the analogy well. 'Love', she says, 'doesn't just sit there like a stone. It has to be made, like bread, remade all the time, made new'. This is true when building a connect between the giver and the receiver. There has to be a sharing of positive emotions, and both would probably need to share experiences from their own lives to find the connect with each other. In a sense, there is a heliotropic effect in humans,

---

[22] 'Emotional intelligence includes the ability to engage in sophisticated information processing about one's own and others' emotions and the ability to use this information as a guide to thinking and behavior. That is, individuals high in emotional intelligence pay attention to, use, understand, and manage emotions, and these skills serve adaptive functions that potentially benefit themselves and others' (Mayer et al. 2008).

[23] A model developed by Peter Salovey and John Mayer.

where we stretch ourselves and emotionally move towards sources of positivity, and flourish when we get enough of it.[24]

There is a risk in exposing your emotions to other people in a deep way, particularly if they are strangers to begin with. Often the hurt one feels through empathy is deep, and different people have different ways to dealing with it, from closing themselves up or embracing all the emotions. All the ways are appropriate, and there is no right way or wrong way. But, in helping others, in allowing your altruistic self to take charge, you must not be a dilatant. Either dive right in, experience whatever you have to, but get down to the work you need to do. Otherwise, it is just a bunch of fancy thoughts and armchair statements.

The way we invest our time and effort in people, more so than merely our money, is an investment in positive emotions and it changes who we are. This happens over time, of course, but it not only has a deeper impact on the receiver, but also has a significant influence on the giver. Sometimes, altruism becomes a way of life for some people, a passion, something that they really value and spend a lot of time with. But at whatever level altruism is brought along with the right emotions, there is the slight increase in positivity. Over time, a deeper change can be seen. The small increases in positive emotions add up and become a key strength in people's lives. Steven Covey uses this idea in leadership development by calling this a deposit in an Emotional Bank Account. The idea, however, is more than a transaction. It is a social resource, a connection between people, a feeling. It even presents itself physiologically, with the psychological resilience leading with a better immunity against common ailments and infections, hinting at an enhanced immune system.

The gradual build-up of positive emotions leads to an improved perception that life is good, and this satisfaction is matched by a

---

[24] The analogy is drawn, of course, from the heliotropic effect in plants, where plants know that sunlight is beneficial to them, and they move and stretch to get as much sunlight as they can.

decrease in depression. It makes us better versions of ourselves. Giving and altruism in any form and to any extent make us look beyond our problems and connect with others and perhaps with wider social needs. We relook at life, making it seem that little bit more worthwhile. And as we extend our reach and help more and more people, and connect more deeply with them, the transaction changes us in deep and meaningful ways.

This is a two-way street! People who experience positive emotions become more helpful to others. Yet being helpful not only springs from positive emotions, it also produces positive emotions. People who give help, for instance, can feel proud of their good deeds and so experience continued good feelings. Additionally, people who receive help can feel grateful, and those who merely witness good deeds can feel elevated. Each of the positive emotions of pride, gratitude and elevation can, in turn, broaden people's minds and inspire further altruistic acts.

It is the power of suggestion, of seeing someone else do an altruistic act. That becomes the source for other people, when they are feeling positive and giving, to extend themselves rather than sit back passively and let the feeling pass. The momentary feeling of gratefulness in one's life can be a mere reflection and then is soon gone. But, seeing someone else can encourage you to find a way to give back. Recognizing kindness and generosity inspires further kindness and generosity. It inspires because altruism sees the best of human character on display, with no holding back by the selfish gene or social considerations.

At other times, a negative emotion can spark a burst of altruistic behaviour, with a person bursting out and screaming that life will be different and the patterns of one's own life will not be repeated. Positivity steps in with a whisper, channelling grief and despair and turning it into powerful tools for service and giving. In the middle of the grief, a voice will whisper about the things that are good; listen to this voice, really listen, because there is a lot of good in everyone's life. Whereas negative emotions are really about the present time, and sometimes the past, positive emotions are really about future time future and about engaging in something larger.

But our ability to kind of use our strengths to transition through and adapt to that new context is key.

There are transformative role models, who serve as exemplars by the strength and power of the good they do for others. Mother Teresa and her Missionaries of Charity, for instance. They wanted to uplift and live the values and service to others that she exemplified. And that sort of aspiring to one's own excellence in seeing another person's excellence is really what's going on with, with inspiration.

This is another more cognitive positive emotion, awe. It is the feeling that you are in the presence of greatness, something quite but greatness on a large scale. While inspiration may affect one individual, it is personal, awe has the ability to affect many people at the same time. It has the power of change on a large scale. The giver can also feel part of a larger whole, be knitted into a larger purpose. This feeling has a deep lesson for charities, as there is an inflexion point beyond which its inspiring acts are regarded as awesome. When that transition happens, the charity becomes truly self-sustaining and will continue to grow.

Negative emotions, including anger and frustration, lead to us assigning blame for things that happen to us, for things that go wrong. The blame can be on individuals we know, on people we do not on circumstances, on God, on each other. But it does not matter, because when the blame game takes over, the person is caught in a negative cycle. But do remember that the reverse can also happen. It can be true for positive emotions as well, that an upward spiral is created, where gratitude takes hold.

Thus, it is important to understand the dynamics of emotions, that they can take you upwards or downwards in a spiral and that the emotions of one moment affect the next. The way out of a downward spiral and the way to enhance an upward spiral are the same. Use cognition and awareness of what is happening to you to cycle emotions into a positive frame. Positive meaning can be found by recognizing benefits within adversity, by giving ordinary events deep meaning and by effective problem-solving. Benefits could include focussing on newfound strengths and resolve within yourself and others. You can infuse ordinary events with meaning by expressing appreciation, love and gratitude even for simple things. And problem-solving and reaching out to people who need your help can actively lead and leverage the benefits of a positive, upward spiral.

The mind can be a powerful ally, and it can take us up or down, so perhaps it is better to think about the good in the world!

As John Milton said, 'The mind is its own place, and in itself can make a heaven of hell, a hell of heaven'.

The new science of positive psychology is beginning to unravel how such transformations can take place. Thinking about goodness cannot only change your life and that of your community, but perhaps also the world.

Keira: 'My grandmother is very religious; she is really wonderful. She looks after our maid so well. Yet, I feel bad because I saw the maid crying; my grandmother lost her temper this morning. Does it make her less wonderful'.

Rita: 'No, it doesn't because there is a difference between empathy and sympathy. You tell me what you think?'

Keira: 'I finally get it. The way we invest our time and effort in people, more so than merely our money, is an investment in positive emotions and it changes who we are'.

Rita: 'You are getting smarter every day'.

RAIN IN THE TIME OF DROUGHT

The moment you doubt whether you can fly, you cease forever to be able to do it.
—J. M. Bar

Jalgaon is a sleepy town in a district in the state of Maharashtra. Nandini is the second child of a couple living there. Nothing much seems to happen in Jalgaon. It is one of the hottest places in India, and the summers are unbearable. But it is home and loved by the people of the area.

Nandini was a lovely child but would fall ill very often. The slightest change in weather would bother her. Viral, mosquito bites, dust and mites including infection of any sort would affect her. They lived in a poor *basti* (locality) where the drains over flowed, people defecated in the open and dogs wandered close to where they stayed in an overcrowded building.

The parents were convinced that if the wind blew in the opposite direction, Nandini would fall ill. Her constant ill health bothered her parents but did not worry them. Her parents would take her to local doctors who would medicate her, and then they would get on with life. Her mother, Nilima, does not work. She has three children to look after at home. Her father, Gulab, is a carpenter and earns about ₹4,000 a month, with which he supports his large family.

Nandini's frequent bouts of illness affected not only her attendance but also her morale in school. She would have struggled for some more time had it not been for a fortuitous coincidence. Doctors from Jupiter Hospital conducted an outreach programme and Nandini happened to be amongst those checked by its medical team. They recommended that she went to Mumbai, as their preliminary evaluation pointed to the need for further tests.

The young girl had been diagnosed with a CHD, in which the septal and posterior leaflets of the tricuspid valve are displaced towards the apex of the right ventricle of the heart. The surgery to repair the tricuspid valve would be scheduled at Jupiter Hospital in Mumbai.

Her parents took the advice of the doctors in the outreach programme and somehow travelled to Mumbai where a panel of specialists further evaluated Nandini's case, and extensive tests were conducted.

The couple was devastated when they were told that surgery was the only way Nandini's life could be saved. A doctor empathizing with their plight told them to focus on the present. Quoting the Buddha, he said, 'The secret of health for both mind and body is not to mourn for the past, not to worry about the future, or not to anticipate troubles, but to live the present moment wisely and earnestly'.

Easier said than done. Without surgical intervention she would collapse soon and may lose her life.

As happens far too rarely in India, it was the doctors from Jupiter Hospital who reached out to a charitable foundation to financially support this case. They were convinced that

Nilima and Gulab could not afford the surgery. And without the operation, there was little hope that Nandini would live long.

Nandini was operated on with a free valve donated from Medtronic India. While she was admitted to the ICU, she developed a complete heart block, so a pacemaker was implanted. Her recovery was further slowed down but her parents kept vigil and buoyed her flagging spirit. The pain was too much for her to bear, and the parents were often reduced to tears seeing her discomfort.

The parents took turns in being beside their daughter. Gulab had the additional pressure of earning so that he could contribute towards the miscellaneous expenditure of being in a big city. Especially since her hospital stay was long, nearly three weeks.

She was discharged in a stable condition and over time has been able to join school. She is now in Senior School. After the surgery, the parents observed a growth spurt. Nandini blossomed after the surgery, gaining height and confidence. She knows life is precious and strives to make the most of each passing day. Her enthusiasm is infectious, and she is extremely popular at school. She understands that her life was saved by prompt medical treatment but retains a sense of humour, regaling her friends with stories of the big city hospital.

She is aware that the nightmare is not over and that she will require another surgery, for which she is on a long-term follow-up.

But as she often tells her mother, 'Regrets will not change the past and worrying won't make me better'. Wise words for a girl her age but not surprising because she has seen so much so soon.

'When I need surgery, somehow things will work out', she assures her parents when they panic if she doesn't look well.

10
GIVING GRATITUDE

We can do no great things; only small things with great love.
—Mother Teresa

There are charitable foundations that are doing excellent work themselves but are grateful to the help and support they get. They recognize that good work is essential, but they are grateful for the environment they work, that supports them, and this makes their work bigger than a job. They feel they are making a real difference to people, putting them back on their feet, and this recognition uplifts them and motivates them to keep going even when the going gets tough. They have worked hard, but they always ensure that they keep themselves mindful of gratitude.

This reflection and thankfulness, on the part of those doing some of the best work themselves, gives hope that the upward cycle of positive emotions will grow in the world. Evidence supports an important asymmetry between positive and negative experiences, called the positivity offset. Positive experiences in lives, it is found, are actually more frequent than negative. Repeated surveys have shown that the statistical evidence is unambiguous; in the distribution of good and bad things happening in people's lives, the statistics favours the good. This gives a tremendous sense of hope and a source of courage. There are just many more good things going on! Now, we need to use gratitude to let those positive events become positive emotions.

Gratitude, for the giver as well as the receiver, enables both to view the world through the positive emotion rather than the material aspect of what is being received, and thereby enables people to feel attached to something larger than themselves. Feeling attached to something larger than oneself builds resilience, and gratitude is one expression of building and being attached to something larger than yourself.

Mindfulness, for all the good and a little of the bad press it has got, is another expression of attaching to a larger purpose. Being mindful implies walking through your day noticing things around you, savouring the beauty of the moment, keeping attached to the world ... being mindful.

If, alongside mindfulness, you were also to be grateful, the combination of gratitude and mindfulness becomes very powerful indeed. Noticing what you have and being grateful for what you already have and are receiving bring a feeling of contentment. With a lens of gratitude, what we already have might feel enough, and so our materialism goes down. Materialism goes down, and humility goes up with gratitude. This works as much for children in refugee camps, happy to have escaped perhaps a war zone, as much as for those privileged enough to lead normal lives.

Gratitude is powerful. It is not self-deprecatory, for in admitting gratefulness to others you are merely widening the altruism in the world, and not taking anything away from yourself. Gratitude is not thinking less of yourself, putting yourself down. Gratitude is thinking of others more, opening your perspective to notice others in the world and what you are receiving from them.

Charities use gratitude effectively if they want to increase their donor base, for it is known that gratitude increases helping behaviour. So, expressing gratitude to a donor means that they are more likely to help again. This extends even further to causes where there are multiple steps in the process; there are donors, helpers accessing the donors and the end-users, that is, the charities. Fundraising in such a situation, which is actually the norm, requires the charities to reach out to the helpers who in turn are reaching out to the donors. The helpers could be teachers helping students reach out to parents, or it may be CEOs reaching out to the companies and boards on behalf of a charity. Sometimes, and surprisingly not often enough, the helpers are genuinely and sincerely thanked for their efforts. Not only the donors, but the helpers as well. Research has found that those charities that were genuine in their gratitude to the helpers raised far more money than those that focused only in thanking their donors. People who are thanked are not only more likely to help the person who is thanking them, but they are also more likely to help someone else. Expressions of gratitude lead to more helping behaviour for the person who was being thanked, but it also has a forward and onward effect, which is important.

If there are so many positives associated with gratitude and being thankful does not cost anyone anything, then why doesn't everyone do it? Why hasn't natural selection led to charities and altruists who are truly grateful to those that help them?

The answer is that gratitude is not always easy. There are some people who express thanks, but they are distracted and do not really notice what they are receiving, and therefore are unaware what they are being thankful for. That is not gratitude. It is not a series of words in a boilerplate email sent to all those who helped with a campaign.

Personal gratitude, privately expressed, is easier. We give thanks to God through prayer, or meditation, or silent thanks on our lips when an accident is avoided. We thank people routinely throughout the day ... but we rarely look them in the eyes or notice who they are. Is this true gratitude?

Gratitude is a little trickier. Deep gratitude involves mindfulness rather than superficiality. One needs to notice how other people are positively impacting you and what you are receiving. It is then that you can express your gratitude to those people.

You can then express gratitude genuinely, without feeling uncomfortable, or vulnerable.

Let us now use the ideas of positive psychology, mindfulness and gratitude to see how to make these your signature character strengths, be deliberate in the way you use the best of who you are to help yourself overcome challenges. Altruism must have this goal, of helping people overcome challenges rather than of overcoming the challenges for them.

Positive psychology is based on the fundamental insight that treating mental illness is not the same thing as promoting mental health. Getting rid of what we do not want in our lives does not automatically bring what we do want.

Similarly, the basic sense of the positive is pretty easy to understand. It is not just the absence of the negative, it refers to things we value, such as joy, courage, optimism, altruism, peace, perseverance, creativity and love. And these things do not automatically come by fighting against sadness, anxiety, fear, selfishness, boredom and hatred, they have to be cultivated and nurtured. Things get rather complex though, once we move beyond a basic understanding of positive in positive psychology. In part, this is because it is difficult to separate the positive from the negative in our lives. And we sometimes label something as negative which, looking back on it later, could be labelled as positive. Conversely, there could also be things that seemed positive at the time, but now you sincerely regret doing.

Some negative experiences lead to positive outcomes and some positive experiences lead to negative outcomes. Even traumatic events can sometimes lead to great personal development, to what researchers call post-traumatic growth.

There are the common effects of positive emotions, and psychology has long understood the value of negative emotions. How anger helps us, how anxiety helps us, how sadness even can help us. But understanding the true worth of positive emotions was more difficult than writing it off as 'feeling good'.

Until a couple of decades ago, psychologists did not really understand what good are positive emotions. Positive emotions did not fit the existing models of emotions, and a new model was required. Fredrickson[25] suggests in her paper 'What Good Are Positive Emotions?' that 'positive emotions serve to broaden an individual's momentary thought–action repertoire, which in turn has the effect of building that individual's physical, intellectual, and social resources'.

Compared with negative ones, positive emotions are relatively fewer, with one for every three or four negative emotions identified. Second, psychology as a discipline did not really care for positive emotions, gravitating towards negative emotions with the inherent problems and issues to confront and solve. Finally, theoretical psychologists built general theories of emotions and used fear and anger as generalized prototypes. As a consequence, the study of positive emotions was neglected.

Fredrickson considered four different positive emotions: joy, interest, contentment and love. She chose these emotions because they appeared to be distinct from one another, and because they appeared to be recognizable across cultures. Her work, therefore, has implications for altruism across the world.

This seminal work suggests that positive emotions 'broaden and build', that they 'broaden (rather than narrow) an individual's thought–action repertoire, with joy creating the urge to play, interest the urge to explore, contentment the urge to savour and integrate, and love a recurrent cycle of each of these urges'.

She argues that there is a propensity to experience positive emotions, and human nature has evolved to use these emotions for individual and collective well-being. Assuming that altruism seeks to assist those in need of help and build greater resilience, there are at least six benefits identified in Fredrickson's work that

---

[25] Professor Barbara Lee Fredrickson is the Kenan Distinguished Professor of Psychology at the University of North Carolina at Chapel Hill.

are useful for the understanding of how marginalized and adversely affected people can be helped through positive emotions.

Positive emotions can broaden the attention span of people, it can help them understand better ('broaden the scope of cognition'), give them a greater locus of control and scope of action, build their physical strength, enhance the intellect and make them more able to deal with and harness social resources. All these are useful and necessary elements in ensuring the lasting benefits accrue to people through philanthropic activities.

As a wholly acceptable side effect, positive emotions can also ameliorate and undo some of the after-effects of negative emotions and may also enhance the health of people. They broaden our awareness and they help us to be more creative and more cognitively flexible. Mental agility and cognitive flexibility help us to stay resilient.

Related to positive emotions and able to enhance the feeling are the benefits from cultivating an attitude of gratitude. This is about sustained gratitude, the practice of being mindful and being truly grateful, rather than getting a momentary feeling of gratitude occasionally. We have seen that people who cultivate gratitude are able to deal with issues better due to enhanced physical and mental health.

Let us contrast this with people who focus on fears, dangers and threats. They are looking for catastrophes and often, through their fearful actions, create the very danger or realize the very threat that they feared. Even if the worst does not happen, it generates an unhealthy level of anxiety.

Gratitude is the opposite of fearing the worst, because in developing an attitude of gratitude you are focussing on what you are receiving, the benefits you are getting, and what is positive. It's a different approach to life.

Seligman and his graduate student studied the effects of gratitude through a randomized online study. They had a control group and a study group. Both groups were required to write a journal with their early memories. There was a difference in the instructions given to the two groups. The control group was asked to merely write about their childhood memories, anything they wanted. The study group was asked to record three positive things that had happened to them and, most importantly, to reflect and think about why those things happened. The experiment was repeated for a week, more to embed the thinking process in the minds of the participants than for any other reason. At the end of the week, both groups were tested on a happiness index as well as on a measure looking for symptoms of depression. What they found is that the people who were in the study group showed increases in happiness compared with the people in the control group who were generally writing about childhood memories.

While a week does not cause long-term behavioural changes, the experiment showed that increases in happiness and decreases in the propensity for depression could be caused by sustained gratitude, for that was what the study group had been asked to do.

Of course, if someone is facing severe depression, then writing a journal is not going to take that feeling away. But it is important for altruists to know that merely providing sustenance and help is not enough. There must be a follow-up on the positive emotional front and structured interventions for people to feel grateful for their lives. These will lead to positive outcomes from the work of philanthropy and also lead to stronger relationships, which may further enhance the warm glow and produce a positive feedback loop.

Keira: 'If there are so many positives associated with gratitude and being thankful does not cost anyone anything, then why doesn't everyone do it? I don't give money any more, but used to give food to the old man near my house. Now, I give it to another person because he thanks me profusely and always has something nice to say'.

Rita: 'That is because the new person shows you gratitude and appreciation, both are powerful emotions'.

'Some people feel entitled and don't get to see beyond their immediate. Each person can start by asking where he or she stands on the spectrum of gratitude and self-centredness'.

THE HEART THAT PUMPED DREAMS

Be quiet so that life may speak.
—Leo Babauta

Kozhikode, or Calicut, is a city in the state of Kerala in southern India. It is the second-largest urban area in the state.

Alka is a four-year-old girl from a remote village in the area surrounding Kozhikode. She was born in October 2012, and her mother, Soumya, was delighted when she held her for the first time.

At a routine medical check on the day after her birth, she was detected with a heart murmur and cyanosis. Simply put, Alka was diagnosed with a CHD. The exact name of the disease is known as an Ebstein's anomaly of the tricuspid valve.

The parents were devastated, and this was their first child. This was a mortal blow and unexpected. Their dreams of taking the baby home and the party that they had planned were aborted as the doctor spoke with them and explained the medical condition.

They were in shock and unable to comprehend the enormity of the situation. What did get through to them though was the precarious nature of the illness and that their child would need regular check-ups. They were informed in no uncertain terms that her health was a priority and needed long-term medical intervention.

The doctors recommended regular follow-up at Calicut Medical College, where she was seen by a senior paediatric cardiologist and a surgeon from the Amrita Institute of Medical Sciences, during a monthly outreach programme. The camp was being conducted at Calicut Ashram in January 2017, after which she was referred to the Amrita Institute for further medical care and management.

Alka wasn't active, she tired easily. Her growth was retarded; she was smaller and more delicate than children her age. Her father, Bijish, is a carpenter and earns ₹250 a day when he has work. Work, however, is erratic and depends on whether he gets a job or task on a particular day or not.

Driven to despair, he borrowed ₹50,000 from a money-lender at an extremely high interest rate. The couple were determined to do what it took to save their little baby.

They finally reached Amrita Institute, in Kochi, in January 2017, where Dr Shine Kumar confirmed the diagnosis. In a joined cardiac conference that was conducted amongst paediatric cardiologists and surgeons; they decided to do a tricuspid valve repair for the little girl.

When both parents were counselled about the surgery, they were explicitly told that without the surgery, their daughter's chances of survival were negligible. That if she were to see the year end, it would be a miracle.

Bijish extended his arm and opened his fist. He was clutching the money he had borrowed but it was not enough.

The doctors made a few calls and were able to put together the required amount with the help of philanthropists. They took on the case on a cost-only basis and helped ease financial burden the family was facing, and thereby ensured that Alka received the surgery required to live.

Bijish left the hospital with his wife and recuperating daughter. This story has a happy ending.

Alka is now in school and in the first grade. After the surgery, she can participate in activities and enjoys herself. An avid reader, she has her nose stuck to a book even in the recess. She loves to sing and is constantly turning the music louder on Bijish's mobile.

Soumya loves to see her little Alka sing along to popular Bollywood songs and rushes to burn dried red chillies to ward away the evil eye. She is certain that her daughter will be a popular singer someday.

They have moved to a better locality where Alka and her parents are not only more comfortable but are local celebrities for saving and nurturing a girl child.

OPTIMISM AS ART OF LIVING

How we spend our days is, of course, how we spend our lives.
—Anne Dillard

When you are stuck in a bad situation that could undermine the strongest, your attitude makes the difference as to whether you will succumb or survive. How do some people have hope while others give up? How can some people find meaning in their lives, whatever the context might be, and how can you continue to find that life is worth living?

Early research on learned helplessness showed that bad or traumatic events do not, in themselves, produce helplessness. Learned helplessness occurs when people or animals feel helpless to avoid negative situations. Martin Seligman first observed learned helplessness when he was doing experiments on dogs. He noticed that the dogs did not try to escape the shocks if they had been conditioned to believe that they could not escape.

The crucial factor is a sense of inescapable trauma. In learnt helplessness, a person has learnt that when bad things happen, nothing they do matters or can change their situation. They give up and remain passive, even after conditions change and they do once again have control over the environment. By then, they have given up hope, so they remain helpless.

The reality of the situation does not affect a person as much as the perception of that reality. The extent to which a person believes bad events will remain stable in time, whether permanently or temporarily, and also if these bad events are locally cited or occur to everyone, determines the reaction of the person and if they have hope or not.

The pessimists believe that the worst will happen. For them, when something bad happens, no matter whether big or small, they instinctively believe that to be part of a chronic pattern and that the bad state would continue forever. Nothing, they believe, will change the situation, and the locus of control is external, so the process is uncontrollable. Some even feel that all they have done in the past will be undone by the bad phase they are going through.

The optimists also go through bad phases, but their reaction is different. First, they believe that the bad times are temporary, so they have hope for the future. Second, they do not make their immediate concerns universal, cutting across all aspects of their lives, or everywhere and at all times. Thus, they retain some semblance of control even under extremely trying circumstances and feel that they can do something about their lives. They have hope.

It is obvious that the pessimists would be more prone to helplessness and would, when bad events occurred, head towards shutting down their lives.

We have seen that positive emotions lead to better well-being, health and good relationships. It is not clear that the same must apply to optimism, for this is a view on a present and future state and not an emotional reaction. Optimism and pessimism are ways of thinking, your belief about the future and beliefs about why bad and good things have happened to you. They are just a single attitude, not a range of feelings and reactions as seen in positive and negative emotions.

However, studies show that optimism is a good predictor for better physical health, longer life, better relationships and better mental health. There is no good reason why a single attitude should predict a variety of psychological and physiological reactions in human beings.

Yet, it does do so.

To understand what is happening and make sense of it in our journey of altruism, we need to look at optimism more deeply. It turns out that optimism is not a single attitude; it is a complex web of beliefs and thoughts that have a behavioural impact on us. It seems that these might be able to drive our feelings and emotions and thereby have an impact on our well-being.

Meaningful interventions for people in need might be well served by looking at the determinants of optimism, as it is easier to be optimistic and show people a brighter future than to take the longer path of creating positive emotions, though the latter has a deeper and more permanent impact. A central question for behavioural theorists to answer is: What are the behaviours that optimists are engaging in, that maybe pessimists are not, and it's those behaviours that are driving all of those really important bottom-line outcomes?

Studies have been done that look at not just the outcomes from optimism, but also the mechanisms that operate and what the functional behaviour patterns are. One of the strongest differences that emerges is that strong optimists are cognitively better adapted, have a more perceptive view of reality, so that they are better able to identify problems than those less optimistic than them. This seems to be a key skill, the ability to identify the problem. The next step in the process is a little bit of a leap of faith; assume for a moment that having successfully identified the problem, you can effect change and therefore reach a good outcome. This claim from the studies is a little bit of a stretch in the logic, for it does not necessarily follow that identification of the problem automatically leads to its solution. Therein perhaps lies one root cause for depression too, when a person has identified a problem and is frustrated at not being able to solve it.

There are other factors involved that are together more recognizable as trend indicators. Optimists are more likely to see a situation as a challenge, not a threat. If they face a negative situation, the instinct is to see it as a threat and then it starts to become overwhelming. The person is unable to cope and starts to go down into a negative emotional cycle. However, an optimist recognizes the situation, accepts it and then sees it as a challenge. Once solving the problem has become a challenge, the energies are positive, and the optimist brings to bear their resources, including their skills and abilities and those of others they can draw upon, in order to find a solution. Whether the skills and abilities actually exist or not, the optimist is able to perceive the situation as a challenge (rather than a threat) and bring to bear behaviours that give the person the best chance of success.

A further difference is that optimists have a good sense of their locus of control and areas of influence. They can identify what they can control, what behaviours they can influence, what leverage they can bring to bear in a situation. Often, not always, they can break down a problem into parts, some of which they are, then, able to solve with their skills and behaviours. Pessimists, on the other hand, might also be able to break down a problem into its parts, but they will focus on the parts that they cannot solve. Optimists are better at accepting that there are aspects that they can do nothing about, and then going about the bits that they can positively change. Pessimists bemoan the bits they can do nothing about and remain in a negative feedback loop around the unfixable.

Besides the cognitive aspects, there are behavioural differences between optimists and pessimists as well. Optimists tend to be more approach oriented and engage with the problems they face. They are always thinking of strategies to change their situation and affect the problem. Pessimists tend to avoid the problems, withdraw from them and quickly cease to engage with potential solutions. An approach orientation, an orientation that leads you to step in and find solutions, is probably going to lead to better outcomes than an orientation where you withdraw.

Optimists are more open than pessimists to get more information, either about the problem or in exploring potential solutions. They seek out information. To get that information, they need to reach out to people and widen their support group. By reaching out, they are likely to receive greater support than pessimists who withdraw into themselves. This difference alone can contribute to some of those outcome differences mentioned earlier.

The next step for optimists is even more effective, as they seem to be more inclined to take action as compared with people who are more pessimistic. They do not just seek information, but they used that information to their advantage.

At the emotional level too, there are differences between optimists and pessimists, but the research evidence to back up this claim is limited, even though it seems to be intuitively correct. Optimists tend to have more positive emotions overall, and we have seen earlier that positive emotions lead to greater resilience. The coping strategies that optimists use are also more effective and have positive outcomes for mental health and emotional health.

Anecdotally, optimists tend to have a better sense of humour than pessimists; they follow exercise routines that they stick with, and they tend to eat more healthily. All these obviously lead to better lives and better outcomes.

Therefore, while optimism is a single attitude, it comes with an associated set of cognitive inclinations and behavioural attributes that can affect health, relationships and can lead to positive outcomes for optimists. By taking purposeful action, the optimist is going to be more likely to live compared with the pessimist. This is a belief system, but the difference between optimism and pessimism affects your resilience; it affects your ability to struggle through difficult times.

Keira: 'I cannot go back to the orphanage, the little girl I played with succumbed to dengue'.

Rita: 'You must be brave to go back when you are ready. Think about her friends, they miss her and now you. In life, our attitude makes a real difference. Some people have hope while others give up, and children learn from what is going on around them'.

POWER OF HOPE AMIDST NO OPTION

Sometimes people are beautiful. Not in looks. Not in what they say. Just in what they are.
—Markus Zusak,
I Am the Messenger

Seven-month-old Yash is the second child born to Jaideep and Samruddhi. They live close to one of Mumbai's most crowded chawls. He was brought to the cardiology evaluation unit because his breathing was laboured. It was visible that he was finding it difficult to breathe and needed to be held for hours before he fell asleep. He could not retain milk and often turned his head away, refusing to feed.

Yash was not gaining weight, and he would cry continuously. All disturbing signs but not alarming since they had an older child and presumed that Yash was just weaker but would catch up.

His paediatrician, however, suspected a heart disease and therefore referred the baby to Jupiter Hospital for an evaluation. The cardiology team examined Yash during one of their outreach OPDs at Dombivili, Maharashtra, where the doctor performed an echocardiogram. It was a huge shock for both the family and the referring paediatricians when the diagnosis was made. Yash was found to have a very complex heart lesion. In medical jargon, aortopulmonary window, also known as type I aortopulmonary window, is one of the very complex heart disorders in children.

In this condition, in medical terms, there is a large communication between the two large blood vessels of the heart, because of which the oxygenated blood recirculates in the lungs. All body functions are laboured because the entire system must work over twice as hard to compensate for this wasted recirculation and this is what stunts normal growth. Pulmonary hypertension, meaning increased pressure within the lungs, is a major complication. It needs immediate surgery.

If that was not enough, Yash had another difficult complication. His heart pumped blood at a reduced level. This condition is referred to as ejection fraction and was a mere 30 per cent and that put him into a high-risk category.

No time could be lost; he needed surgery at once. The parents were not in a situation to understand either the complexity of the lesion, the urgency for operation or the risks associated with it.

To complicate issues further, they had no money to fund the expensive operation. Jaideep works as a peon in a private school, and his annual income at that time was less than ₹40,000.

What they lacked in money, they made up for in love and determination. They were ready to do anything to ensure that their child got the surgery he needed.

Yash was immediately started on medications in the hope that his heart pumping function would improve, while the parents ran around trying to raise funds for his medical care. Strangers came to their help, and the doctors referred them to philanthropists. The family would never know and did not understand why those who did not know them at all were willing to extend such vast sums of money to pay for the medical bills of their son.

Initially it was thought that the surgery could be performed with an AP window device closure, which means correcting the lesion without open-heart operation, which significantly reduces the risk of the procedure for the baby in view of ventricular dysfunction (low pumping function). But, miraculously, the heart function showed an improving trend and responded to medications. At the time of admission, Yash had normal heart function and needed urgent surgery to close the defect.

The surgery was performed at Jupiter Hospital by the best surgical team. An open-heart operation was needed to close the defect and the baby had a good recovery after surgery. At present, the child has been taken off major life support systems and medications and he is recovering on his own.

Yash has celebrated his first birthday in November 2018, and he has just started to walk. He is now meeting milestones in growth and development despite being born with an extremely complex and rare heart disorder.

12
GRIT, FOCUS AND DETERMINATION

Regrets are as personal as fingerprints.
—Margaret Culkin Banning

Philanthropists have limited resources, charitable causes are greater than the charity can provide for, and altruism has its limitations. In a world where limited resources are chasing increasingly wider and deeper problems, there is some selection that gets done as to who gets helped and who doesn't. Some causes are in themselves widely publicized and keep getting supported, while others are thought to be more basic in the survival game. Ultimately, the decision taken by donors and altruists is based on their perception of where the limited resources will have the greatest impact. Grit and focus are the differentiators that donors look for, but the problem lies in predicting who will win the game of getting the help from altruists.

Research has tried to answer the question that other than talent and opportunity, what makes some people more successful than others. This is critically important for donors, as they are keen to put their money into organizations that will be successful in meeting their goals and ambitions. It has been found that one important determinant of success is grit—the tenacious pursuit of a dominant superordinate goal despite setbacks (Duckworth and Gross 2014). Grit implies that an organization will work towards its focused goals, regardless of the obstacles that might be placed in its way. Also, donors are looking for organizations that can sustain themselves over years or even decades, and this requires grit and determination. As Duckworth and Gross show, in contest and conflict situations, the winners in most cases are those with the greatest grit and self-discipline. If you want systemic change in problem areas, you need to find the people with grit and resilience who can get the job done. If you are looking at helping a child survive a disease, look for the gritty, resilient kid, the one who will fight for his/her life and help you help him/her.

Understanding this sentiment and the motivations of donors can help NGOs and others seeking philanthropic support. While, in an ideal world, altruism should extend to all those who are needy, in reality it is those who fight with all their spirit who end up winning the support of philanthropists.

It is possible to assist people to be more optimistic, to be more positive and to develop a fighting spirit. It involves both hope and courage. Hope lies in the future, so the need is to show the receivers of aid that all is not lost and that the future can be better for them. Courage comes from accepting the reality of the present, and then using it as a base for moving ahead. You need to manipulate the past and the present to deal with depression and anxiety.

However, depression is fear of the future, a disorder about a state of affairs that has yet to arrive and not about the present or the past. The cognitive triad, as it is known, in depression has three negatives: negative thoughts about the self, negative thoughts about the world and negative thoughts about the future. The really important one is the third, negative thoughts about the future. Depression often occurs when belief in a better future is lost.

The way to deal with people we help, as a complement to our altruistic activities, is to be believable in the better future scenarios we create. Creating future scenarios are like necessary therapies, be they a change in circumstance, location or mental attitude. But they must all look at various possible future scenarios and be able to evaluate them together in order to move ahead. Along the way, anxieties about the future and expectations that things will go wrong will take place. But the basis needs to shift from the past and present to the future in order for it to have hope of success. However, this shift to the future must be accompanied by an acceptance of the present and a removal from the past.

There is a famous psychological experiment called The Gorilla Experiment, in which you are looking at a screen and people are on a basketball court, and they're passing basketballs back and forth. And your job is to count the number of passes. This seems to be easy. As a twist, in the middle of the game, a gorilla (or someone in a gorilla suit) walks across the basketball court.

Now here comes the surprising part. About half the people do not see the gorilla. They do not see the gorilla at all! They do not perceive, they don't observe. But they usually get the number of passes approximately correct.

This issue has to do with our visual perception system. The brain and our optical, visual system are just a bunch of nerve cells. The base of the nerve cells and the visual system in the brain is packed with analysing the light signals that reach the retina. Associated and above that in the brain are more abstract interpretation units, which are also getting some of the signals from the retina but are processing this incomplete new information along with previous information and perhaps memories. As one moves away from the basal visual system in the brain, there are increasingly abstract perceptions being set up. The return message loop carrying instructions about what the eye should look at and focus on is smaller and carries less information than the optic nerve that takes information to the brain. In this process, the brain asks the eyes to amplify signals about the basketball and to reduce or ignore information about gorillas. The previous information and memories reject the idea of a gorilla at a basketball game and refine the perception to recognize the basketball. The visual system is therefore a bit of a hallucination, as what you see is mixed up with the brain's abstract idea of what you should be seeing.

This idea can be extended to other perceptions as well and is not confined only to the visual system. What it effectively says is that the brain can be trained to respond better to optimistic and positive outcomes, and this can be a powerful mechanism for the treatment of anxiety and depression.

Therefore, even in the worst of circumstances, the human spirt and the brain can fight to create a better outcome. Part of the method lies in focussing solely on the immediacy of the problem and ignoring the inconsequential. If, for instance, observers had been asked to look for disruptions to the basketball game instead of counting the number of passes, they may well have spotted the gorilla. Normal life has to be abandoned at a time of crisis or when working for causes that are poorly funded or ill supported. Those who are successful in attracting the attention of philanthropists are those who show focus (on the problem or the issue) and demonstrate grit and determination in doing something about it.

Keira watches Rita sign a cheque and is perplexed. Finally, she can't hold back and asks, 'Why did you give that woman money? How do you know she is raising money for the charity and that she will actually give it?'

Rita: 'I don't know anything more than you do. But her grit and her determination moved me. I gave for that reason'.

THE HOUR OF HAPPINESS

We can't help everyone, but everyone can help someone.
—Ronald Reagan

Michael is the fourth child in his family, who live in the southern Indian state of Tamil Nadu. He belongs to a family of eight, including his parents and five brothers and sisters (three elder and two younger). And his extended family of doting uncles and aunts stay within a stone's throw from his house. His parents, Dhanam and Vadivel, are extremely proud of him.

His mother often describes him as 'a shy child who has grown into a young man but still does not like to talk very much'. However, his otherwise serious face morphs into a big smile when the conversation is about cricket. Like other boys in his class, it was his passion; he loved the sport. He loved watching it as much as playing it. He was chuffed when the Indian team beat other international teams and brought the trophy home. T20 was something he lived for, finishing his homework hours before the match started. He begged his sisters not to talk while he watched the match. They, in turn, would tease him, saying, 'Shall we hold our breath until your match gets over?'

Michael hero-worshipped the cricket all-rounders; being one himself, he identified with them. 'They are all-rounders on the field, whereas I am good at academics and sports', he thought. He always got prizes on his school's annual day.

They say life trips you when you are busy making plans, a cliché that would be appropriate to describe what happened to Michael.

All was well until one fateful day. Michael was in class XI, studying in a good government school in Thanjavur district (Tamil Nadu). He had his goal. He was studying hard to qualify as a chartered accountant. His father points out that he is 'very particular about his things, and the otherwise calm boy is known to lose his temper if anything is out of place on his desk'.

He lived by his favourite quote, which he had posted on his cupboard, 'Happiness, not in another place, but this place... not for another hour, but this hour: Walt Whitman'.

Ironically, all it took was one hour to turn his routine life into a nightmare of hospitals and doctors, bitter medicine and X-rays.

A murmur was detected during a routine school health check-up, an event which was so routine that the parents forgot all about it until Michael came home with the reports.

The doctors had been quite firm; further tests were needed and there was no time to be lost. He had to be taken to the Miot Hospital in Chennai for a better evaluation. The findings of the tests shocked not only Michael's parents but also the doctors. Michael was suffering from a complex inborn heart defect—Ebstein's anomaly—a very rare heart disorder that affects the tricuspid valve (the valve present between the two right chambers of the heart).

As if this wasn't enough to throw the families into disarray and turmoil, the doctors discovered that he also had an ASD, which, simply put, meant there was a large hole in the membrane between the two upper chambers.

The parents were devastated upon being told that an open-heart surgery was the only way to save their child. For Vadivel, a farmer, mustering the enormous sum for the surgery was an impossible dream. He earned ₹4,000 a month. Even with help from his extended family, specially his brother, it was a losing battle.

Every time he returned empty-handed after asking for help, his heart sank when he saw Michael.

And, then, unexpectedly, a charitable foundation came forward and supported the family by paying the medical bills.

Michael underwent surgery and was stable after the operation, responding well to treatment. He was discharged as per schedule and encouraged to lead an active normal life. However, he was cautioned against playing cricket.

Today, Michael has recovered completely and is doing well in school. He does take part in other school activities, is a keen debater and loves to watch Rajnikant's movies.

When his mother fusses over him, he quickly diverts her attention to his brothers and sisters.

13
DEVELOPING THE DRIVE TO DO GOOD

Will and energy sometimes prove greater than either genius or talent or temperament.
—Isadora Duncan

Altruists never doubt that a small group of people can make a change, for they are seized by the drive to make a difference. However, are we always working with the sense of emergency and urgency that is required. We need to now apply the tools we have looked at mainly from the perspectives of the recipients to study the behaviour and not merely the motivations of the givers.

Optimism predicts better physical health, longer life, better relationships and better mental health. And this is not only for the recipient but also for the donor. Optimism is also perceived to be a strong leadership quality, so altruists and particularly those working in the field need to show leadership to change attitudes and defeatism.

Altruists need to be optimists not because it is a panacea. No, it is not. But it is an important part of developing resilience and defences against many of the problems faced by people. It is really good to be naturally optimistic, but for others it has to be developed and nurtured.

Let us take the case of someone who was physically active, a child or an adult, and suddenly it is discovered that he or she had a life-threatening illness. Perhaps, it had been there for some time, perhaps it was recent. This did not matter, and neither did the cause or any aspect that was in the past. Here and now, the illness existed. In this situation, with things going horribly wrong, the twin aspects of optimism and rootedness in the present can be helpful. If the support group around the person is optimistic and positive, the energies flow to the person and, within the bounds of medical possibility, the best outcomes are often obtained. If there is a sense of gratitude and that is also something typical you see in optimists, the reality seeks out the best possible outcomes. Optimists do not look at the negative; they focus on the positive. And they find meaning in their existence, in their daily routine. The altruist can help with the actual treatment, can provide an alternative experience, or do so many other things. But the best that someone can do is create positive emotions through a sense of gratitude and optimism.

Using the techniques that have been described in this book, the behaviour of individuals, social groups and individual motivations can be understood better, so that altruists can direct their energies more effectively. We have talked about positive emotions, how you assess optimism, and we've talked about gratitude and resilience. There are some really important findings that we must recognize. Positive behaviours lead to optimistic thinkers, to people to have increased stress resilience. They cope with stress more effectively, perhaps because they have the belief that the future is bright, so what they are going through today isn't as difficult for them to handle. We also know that people who have greater social support are likely to do better than people who isolate themselves. So, the altruist working with a reclusive person has to bring them out into society as best as they can. Perhaps some people have greater social support even in adverse circumstances because of their attitude and visible positive energy. Altruists can help isolated persons start to develop relationships, though this should not translate into dependency from either side. When you have someone you can lean on, the outcomes can be much more positive.

Another set of studies have looked at how a positive attitude relates to mental and emotional well-being. One of the aims of altruistic interventions is to ensure that people have greater quality of life, and they are happier. They have greater well-being. If your belief is that the future is bright, that might help buffer against feelings of depression too. The research shows that by learning cognitive therapy, which includes learning how to challenge overly pessimistic beliefs, altruists can help reduce depression and increase emotional health, sometimes leading on to improvement in physical health too. There have been many studies done looking at optimism in the domain of physical health. The top finding is that people who are higher on optimism have a better, more robust immune response. That means you are going to be less likely to get sick.

Some people who are adversely impacted by circumstances do not reintegrate into society, but this integration is a key outcome that philanthropy looks at. Success in the real world for those they are helping is the ideal outcome for many altruists. And success can be measured in all sorts of different ways. One important measure is perhaps success at work. Reintegrating marginalized people back into the workforce at any level requires the person to face up to a lot of adversity, a lot of stress and a lot of rejection. Attitudes, resilience and hope for a better future, while being rooted in the present, are the aspects that really matter here too. If you are in a professional situation which involves high stress and high attrition, optimism confers an advantage. Those with positive emotional health are more likely to stay in those high-stress situations, while others may drop out. So, attitudes have really important benefits in terms of success and reintegration into society. But success can be measured in ways other than work as well. Whatever be the metric for the measurement of success for marginalized individuals or communities, the transition from a stressful present, to forgetting the past and developing positive attitudes for the future seems to signpost the path forward.

In most cases of where altruistic activity works over an extended period, people's stress levels are high and emotional strength is way down. Ultimately, we can only control what we can control. And if we think that we are going to be able to control all the other factors around us, we will be totally stressed out all the time, and feel like we are failing, because we cannot solve everything. So, the final learning for altruists is how to understand what you can control, and work on those measures will make you feel a lot happier at the end of the day.

Keira: 'My parents always say most NGOs are defrauding the public; the money is not used for the cause that they ostensibly support. So, I stay away from them as should you'.

Rita: 'I don't think so. I believe there are many out there that impact lives on a daily basis. Research is a must; you must know what your money is being spent on before you give'.

THE SPIRIT OF NEVER GIVING UP

I alone cannot change the world but I can cast a stone across the waters to create many ripples.
—Mother Teresa

Deena was born with a congenital heart condition, diagnosed with VSD at the age of six months when she developed pneumonia. Her parents had taken her to the local government hospital, expecting it to be just another fever, but the doctor noticed breathing problems and an irregular heart murmur.

After being given medicines for the pneumonia, she was referred to another government hospital for further examination. An echocardiograph was performed, and a hole was discovered in the lower chambers of her heart.

Deena was a small baby of six months, so the doctors prescribed medication and advised the parents to wait for at least two years before deciding a further course of medication. This was only the beginning of what turned into an endless cycle of doctors and hospitals.

Born to Satya Prakash, an accountant in a housing society, and his wife Pinki, Deena struggled with problems for years. She wanted to play outside with her twin sister and younger brother. She yearned to take part in games and physical activities with children in the neighbourhood. She looked out of the window longingly as she watched her brother and sister grab their father's hand pulling him towards the gate.

However, the hole in her heart limited physical exertion. Two years later, when the parents took her to the hospital, she was still not ready for the operation according to the attending doctors. They were sent back with instructions on how to care for Deena and told to bring her back a couple of years later for further treatment.

Time passed and Deena joined school. She studied and enjoyed academics, while still longing to go play with children her age. She graduated from nursery to primary school and developed a strong fascination for karate. She spent hours watching it, aware that she would never be allowed to indulge her passion.

Knowing there was no way her heart could support physical activity beyond her daily routine, she turned her attention to academics.

She would sometimes play at home with her twin sister and younger brother, sticking to games they made up. However, no matter how much they tried to include her, she would always be envious of their ability to take part in sports and feel left out.

Deena continued to visit the local hospitals at the right intervals and kept being sent back without so much as a word about a permanent solution.

They say all it takes is a moment for life to change. Deena's world came crashing when, one day, she collapsed at school and had to be rushed to the nearest private hospital, where she was resuscitated.

Luckily, she was discharged soon, with the advice to consult a paediatric cardiologist at the same hospital. The parents were hopeful, finally, of a permanent solution for her suffering and weak heart. Maybe their prayers had been answered.

However, their hopes were as easily dashed as they realized that they would not be able to afford the cost of treatment at a top-class private hospital on their small income of ₹6,000 a month. They would, as it happened, not even be able to afford the doctor's fees, so the operation was a distant dream.

Committed to give it their all, they started seeking help from their extended family. A relative who knew a doctor at Max Hospital, a leading multi-specialty hospital in the country, advised them to visit the hospital.

Sceptical though they were, they went ahead. At Max, an echocardiogram was done and Deena's diagnosis of VSD was confirmed. The doctors found that the hole, fortunately, had good margins and could be closed in the Cath Lab with a device.

The parents were extremely happy with the hope of finally finding an answer, but their joy was short-lived. They could not afford the post-operative cost.

Different parts of the country, different patients, different hospitals—the same story of altruism. But with the hospital reaching out, a prominent charitable foundation provided financial aid. With prompt intervention, Deena's treatment was given a go-ahead, and the procedure was successfully performed on her heart.

Having returned home in much better health, Deena now not only enjoys living her life to the fullest. She now has the health to make even her wildest dreams come true. She has joined karate classes and has received a certification from IIT for the same. She is preparing for the national-level competition now.

Encouraged, Deena dreams big. She wants to become a doctor and save lives. Her medical team are her rock stars. Her parents are happy and support her. They tell her she is an eagle, and the opposing wind will just take her higher.

CREATING 'IMPACT' THROUGH GIVING

There are years that ask questions and years that answer.
—Zora Neale Hurston

Pushpa Sundar, the founder-director of Sampradaan India Centre for Philanthropy, has spent most of the last 30 years researching Indian philanthropy. She realizes that the dominant belief in India has been that social development in society is either for local communities and families to handle, or else a task for government to do. Along with other researchers and commentators, she calls altruistic giving for the love of humanity to be 'one of mankind's noblest instincts'. As we have studied in this book, this instinct is not intrinsic to our molecular biology and is a socially acquired trait, which has resulted in humans being cognitive vastly different to other animals on this planet.

Sundar makes an important distinction between the various forms of altruism, which for the purposes of this book we have taken to be fungible. She says (Sundar 2017):

> Altruistic giving, or giving out of compassion and without expectation of a material return, has been variously described as charity, philanthropy, or social investment. The terms 'charity' and 'philanthropy', in particular, are frequently used interchangeably, but in fact both have different nuances since each evolved at different times and in different contexts.

Charity is the voluntary giving of money to those in need, where the motive is compassion and the desire is to as immediately as possible relieve distress. It does not seek to address root causes, is highly directed and takes a short-term perspective. Charity does not usually seek to reduce social ills or make a more socially homogeneous country.

Philanthropy is for the transformation of society, where there is long-term planning by the altruist to identify, tackle and cure the ills of society. The difference with charity, other than the usual size of donations and the time frame involved which vary a lot, is really in the nature of how the altruism is directed, used and for what purpose. Philanthropy has a wider societal purpose than charity, which is more immediately ameliorative.

Indian philanthropy and charity is lower than the proportionate GDP share as compared with most countries. The Charities Aid Foundation has, in its CAF World Giving Index 2018, has ranked 124th out of 144 countries for which data were collected. India, however, comes second to China in the absolute number of people who help strangers. Again, India comes out on top, followed by China and the United States in the absolute number of people who give to charity and those who volunteer their time to charity. When allowance is made for the adult population of India, its ranking plummets to the lowest quartile. It is ranked 136th for helping a stranger, 89th for donating money and 101st for volunteering time. The top-six countries in the rankings are Indonesia, Australia, New Zealand, the United States, Ireland and the UK. The mix of giving, however, and the causes for which it is given do differ, as we also saw in the vast differences between giving in the United States and Britain.

There is a need for greater strategic philanthropy, directed towards specific causes that can have a wider societal impact. At the same time, ameliorate charity affects the lives of people immediately and has a positive, curative effect.

Whatever be the means of giving and the type of altruism a person might want, it seems important to be 'intentional' in one's giving. Knowing who would like to give to is important; otherwise we run around doing good, but not doing right. Just because something sounds like it is a good idea, does not make it so. Each person who wants to help needs to identify the different spheres of relationships (and specific people who are in those spheres) whom they wish to help. Each of those relationships requires different types of giving. Some relationships are mutual and yet are maintained by giving to each other; others are more geared towards one person or group giving to meet a need of the other.

Developing a purposeful plan for giving away money might seem silly. Perhaps you want to give wherever and to whomever you like without feeling constrained by a plan. There is great freedom in that philosophy. However, there are also great dangers. Putting together a purposeful plan for giving is necessary in order to have a sustainable impact.

Giving, whether you have a plan or not, is made easier if you have information about what and how the money will be used by the organization you give to. The importance of informed giving cannot be overstressed. There are two reasons why a donor might give to a charity. First, the charity might be fulfilling the donor's own desires and wishes (and in this form, the charity is acting as an agent for the donor). Second, the charities themselves might have causes that they support and they actively fundraise from donors for these causes (and here the charity advocates a cause to the donor). Donors must understand the nature of the charities' pitch, and specifically whether it is acting as an agent for the donor's wishes or advocating their own causes. In general, it is seen that donors who give regularly are highly influenced by prior knowledge of or affiliation with a charity and are unlikely to respond to random advocacy or solicitation. Prior knowledge and good communication of its works and impact are highly desirable for a charitable organization.

And, finally, the most important question to answer for altruists is what it means to have 'impact' and why it matters. This is a difficult question to answer, for different people will have different definitions of impact. How to make a difference is a matter of your personal philosophy. For some people, this may mean the number of people whose lives you improve, and how much you improve them by (the latter being a process requiring definition, monitoring and evaluation). 'Improving lives' could be thought of in terms of 'increasing well-being', treating everyone as equally valuable. Other altruists might want specific defined outcomes, and measures to ensure that those outcomes have been achieved.

As an altruist, in the broadest practical terms, 'impact' would be the extent to which your contribution to solving social problems helped make the process faster than it would have been otherwise. It might perhaps also include making a wider impact than would otherwise have been possible.

In summary, therefore, altruism would aim for a larger impact either when the problem itself is large or if you make a larger contribution to it.

Motivations, however, will differ. As we have learnt, altruistic behaviour is not inherently in our genes. It has to be learnt. Fortunately, our physical frailties and the powers we gained through language and the Cognitive Revolution have made us capable of societal structures and of working together. Altruism may not be in our genes, but it is very much part of what makes us human beings.

Keira: 'So, giving, whether you have a plan or not, is made easier if you have information about what and how the money will be used by the organization you give to'.

Rita: 'Yes, this is important. Know your cause, know who you are helping'.

After a pause.

Keira: 'Rita, I realize that the power to make a change lies within me. I don't have to rely on undependable news or politically motivated leaders. I can start a change; right here, right now'.

Rita: 'Good. The motivation is not important, the action is'.

AGAINST ALL ODDS

Courage is found in unlikely places.
—J. R. R. Tolkien

Meenu was born into a poor family and lived a life of subsistence. She had a father who had neither a job nor a steady income. Her mother was a young woman without any formal education and was unlettered. The parents had no land nor a home of their own. Her father sold milk to barely make enough to live. The business did not flourish. He had put up a makeshift room on the sidewalk of the market using corrugated tin sheets. This shelter served both as their home and as a shop; it had neither running water nor a toilet. The public water pump in the area was used, and the family lived in this very basic accommodation.

Meenu had an elder brother and a younger sister, and she remembers that when she was about five years old, her father had severely beaten her brother after drinking hooch. She remembers that the boy bled profusely and passed away soon after. Not very much later, her younger sister passed away.

The now reduced family of two parents and Meenu lived together in their home under the tin sheets, and there was constant strife between the parents. Money was always the biggest problem.

A customer who regularly bought milk from her father offered to admit Meenu into the Jaswant Modern School (JMS). He was an executive in one of the bigger banks of the country and posted in Dehradun. This encounter was responsible for Meenu joining the JMS, where children from the Purkal Youth Development Society (PYDS) were also studying. Unfortunately, after a few months, this philanthropic gentleman was transferred out of Dehradun and that was also the end of his financial support to Meenu for her schooling.

It was at this time when the father, who was unable to manage his family, decided to abandon them, marry another woman and leave Dehradun. The mother and daughter were thus left on their own. The mother, uneducated and ill equipped to face the world, attempted feebly to look after her daughter. She tried her hand at the milk-selling business. After struggling for a few weeks, the mother decided to abandon the daughter and move away and live on her own. Meenu has not seen or heard from her since that day.

What was left after these series of sad incidents was the small room made out of corrugated tin sheets, a few debts left behind by the mother for milk, vegetable and provisions and the few pieces of clothing that covered Meenu's back. All the rest had been either pawned or sold away. Meenu was surrounded by petty creditors who threatened her safety. She had no option but to stay in the dark of her room, hungry, facing an uncertain future. The school was threatening to throw her out and there was no way the watchman at the school gate would permit her entry.

Swati was her only friend and had relentlessly pestered and persevered to get Purkal to admit her friend. It is in these circumstances that Swamy, a prominent resident of the town, and a friend of his, Anshu, visited Meenu in her shed at Rajpur. They had been persuaded by Swati. Having no one to turn to and with thoughts of suicide in her head, Meenu had desperately written to Swati on a piece of paper torn out of her school notebook, begging for support and help.

On reaching the shed at Rajpur, what Swamy saw was not what he was prepared for. There were seven to eight tin sheets bound together by a wire and this made for a house. It had no windows. There was another rusted sheet, again bound by a flimsy rope that made for the door. Swamy asked Meenu to open the door, but she wouldn't, as there were three belligerent men standing outside too. Swamy spoke with them, and they said that both her mother and father had fled, leaving this girl behind and that they had a debt of over ₹500 to collect. They were banging at the door and shouting and threatening the girl inside. Not a whimper was to be heard from inside.

With lots of persuasion from Swati, they finally got the door opened. When discovered by Swami and Anshu, Meenu was found hiding desperately, with terror written all over her eyes. They saw inside the dark shed, a young girl about 13 or so, huddled in a corner. She was visibly terrified and sobbing hysterically. It was obvious that she had not eaten for some time.

The petty debt was settled in cash by Swamy, and Meenu could now be removed from the spot to the safety of some home. The critical state of the child's condition moved them so much that she was immediately granted admission to the Purkal school.

Having accepted responsibility for Meenu, a hornet's nest had been disturbed. Meenu, a minor girl, had to be housed and taken care of. Since the school at that time did not have the facility of providing breakfast or dinner, this had to be made possible.

The school not only took care of Meenu's education but rehabilitated her.

Although she started at 25 per cent marks at a base test, her marks improved dramatically with time as she became mentally and emotionally stable. She eventually passed her class XII examinations with 71 per cent marks.

Meenu subsequently graduated as a student of Mass Media from the prestigious DIT University and is a confident young lady. She worked for a while as the caretaker of the newly constructed TATA Hut at PYDS. She later moved to Delhi, where she works in the HR department of a multinational company, and she has also found herself a place to stay.

Within a short span of three years, Meenu has insisted upon and paid to PYDS all the money that was spent on her, saying that there would be other deprived children like her who would need the funds.

EVERY SOUL IS A PHOENIX

Courage is grace under pressure.
—Ernest Hemingway

Seventeen years is how long Lalmati and Mohanlal had waited for a child. Their happiness knew no bounds when Lalmati's pregnancy was confirmed. They could not wait, their excitement was palpable. It seems, neither could he, for their little son was born at 28 weeks, 12 weeks premature.

The premature birth itself was a terrifying ordeal for the family, with their tiny baby weighing only a kilogramme. It meant constant vigilance by doctors attending to him in the intensive care unit. He was being treated in a level III intensive care unit, under the care of vigilant neonatologists. Over the next 23 days, Shyam, as he was named by his parents, continued to lose weight despite tube feeding and the best care by the team of doctors.

He was finally diagnosed as having a heart disorder known as patent ductus arteriosus (PDA). This occurs when there is an unwanted connection between the two major blood vessels of the heart: the aorta and the pulmonary artery. Due to this connection, oxygenated blood from the aorta is shunted into the pulmonary artery, depriving the body of oxygen-rich blood. Thus, these children face health problems which stunted growth. Some children succumb because of further complications.

Shyam's father, Mohanlal, is a migrant labourer from the north of India working in a small private company in Silvassa, Dadra and Nagar Haveli. He could not afford the expensive neonatal intensive care unit (NICU) care at the government hospital, neither could he hope to provide tertiary paediatric care whose expertise is mostly limited to private hospitals with his limited resources.

Shyam's weight had dropped to 900 grams. He was dependent on oxygen provided externally and was being fed via a tube inserted into his stomach via his nostrils. None of the medicines recommended for treating PDA had worked, and the only way forward now seemed to be a surgical procedure.

The couple despaired. They raged against an unfair God. What justice was this, their tired minds cried out. They lost hope and felt defeated.

The medical team, meanwhile, unknown to the couple, had arranged funding through a charitable organization. Immediate financial approvals were given, after which the baby was instantaneously shifted to Jupiter Hospital in Thane.

The baby was admitted to the NICU under a surgeon who specializes in cardiac procedures for such small babies. He has to his credit more than 1,200 successful cardiac catheter interventions. A team of neonatal specialists was put together. A procedure called PDA device closure was performed in February 2018. In this procedure, the heart defect is closed using a highly specialized implant called the PDA device, which is the best process for surgery on such small children. This implant is inserted via a venous port accessed in the baby's thighs. The entire operation was performed with only a needle inserted into the body and without having to cut open the chest. The advantage of this procedure is accelerated recovery and minimal invasion.

Shyam was taken off ventilator within next 18 hours and feeds were introduced immediately after the procedure. He is now stable, and at present recovering in the NICU and is expected to do well.

What makes this case unique is that, at 900 grams, Shyam happens to be the smallest baby in India to undergo PDA device closure. He is a miracle for his parents, but also for the medical fraternity in the country.

As for Shyam's parents, this is a miracle that they had been waiting for 17 years; they are just glad they get to finally take him home.

Now, 10 months later, he is a healthy 4 kg and is a bundle of energy His parents are conscientious about taking him for regular check-ups with the doctor, who conducts an OPD in Silvassa.

They want the best for their son, but for now it is one day at a time. The memories are still raw, and the parents get emotional when they look back on the last year.

LIGHT AT THE END OF A DARK TUNNEL

Act with kindness but do not expect gratitude.
—Confucius

Shahadevan's wife, Selva, had a natural, but premature delivery at around 29 weeks of gestation in July 2017. The baby boy was born at a local hospital, with a low birth weight and breathing problems. The parents were at a loss, and completely unsure of how to proceed thereon. An echo test at the hospital was conducted, which revealed a CHD—VSD—which needed surgery. Shahadevan works in a supermarket and earns ₹8,000 a month and was unable to put together the money required for the surgery.

The owner of the local hospital guided them towards the Amrita Institute of Medical Sciences in Kochi and even organized an ambulance to transport the family, free of cost. This was the beginning of the good will that ensured that their baby would go on to survive.

At the hospital the doctor told the parents that their baby needs to be operated on, but only after he had been stabilized. The biggest challenge, the doctor explained, was that their son was born prematurely, and so he was put on a ventilator in the NICU.

After some time, he was finally operated on, weighing merely 1.5 kg at the time of the surgery. The surgery took place without a problem, and he was in the hospital for two months. He was finally discharged in November 2017.

'My wife and I will never forget what the team at Amrita Institute of Medical Sciences and other charitable foundations have done for us. We went through a great deal during that time. My wife was under medical care for quite some time after the delivery and I was not allowed to take leave for too long from my job. It was with the support of my parents who stood by our baby Param's side that all of this was physically possible. Even with the funds we had, we begged and borrowed from our friends and relatives, and we are not ashamed to admit this as we would have done anything to save our son. We put together a total of just under ₹200,000, but there was still a gap which was filled by others who did not know us at all', said the father of the child.

The baby is now healthy and happy. The child is doing extremely well physically and his parents look forward to sending him to school in time.

WISHING UPON A SHOOTING STAR

Happiness can be found, even in the darkest of times if one only remembers to switch on the light.
—J. K. Rowling

Thanjavur, formerly Tanjore, is in the state of Tamil Nadu and is known as the 'Rice Bowl of Tamil Nadu'. The nearest airport is Tiruchirappalli International Airport and the nearest seaport is Karaikal Port.

Mahesh is the fifth child of Balraj and Mahalakshmi who live on the outskirts of Thanjavur in a small village. When he was nine years old, he fainted during the morning assembly in his school. The teachers panicked and rushed him to the closest government hospital. Routine tests were followed by more detailed ones, and the results were disturbing.

The parents were in a state of shock. Their son appeared normal to them; he actively participated in all school events and played sports.

A screening was done, after which the doctors sat down both parents and counselled them. The diagnosis was that their son had a hole in his heart. The doctor told the parents that it was best to keep him on close observation and hope that the hole closes on its own. This was a possibility that could not be ruled out.

Approximately a month later, at a routine check-up in school, the doctor detected a murmur and referred Mahesh to Miot Hospital in Chennai. The parents took their son for the necessary tests and the echocardiogram revealed that he did indeed have a CHD, and that there were complications. His aortic valve had two leaflets and was severely narrow. A normal aortic valve usually has three leaflets. As a result of this narrowing, less oxygenated blood was flowing through his body. He required an open-heart surgery, but the parents were not going to be able to pay for the medical bills.

They had five children, and Balraj worked as a labourer in a furniture shop and earned ₹4,000 per month. Living every day was difficult. His earnings supported a large family and, therefore, putting together the money for the surgery was impossible for them.

They were under immense pressure. Mahalakshmi was devastated. Life had struck them a mortal blow almost mocking their situation. Penniless and distraught, they did not know whom to turn to.

The doctors at Miot Hospital referred this case to an altruistic group, who agreed to financially support the surgery. The surgery went well, and Mahesh was put on a long-term follow-up.

He recovered and rejoined school with renewed vigour. After the surgery, he is unstoppable. He is always winning the sports events he participates in. As a sprinter, he regularly wins the 100 m and 200 m races in school. He is also an active volleyball player. He plays tournaments and represents his school at not only inter-school but also state-level competitions.

Now in regular school, his heart is set on being a sportsman. He wants to succeed and bring his family and country glory. His parents, however, are worried.

They say, 'We want the best for him and for him to be who he wants to be. However, sports at a professional level scare us after everything that he has endured health-wise. It needs to be health first for him; we are always worried, as there are some limitations. Our son is great at academics too, not just sports—he truly is our little star!'

A HOPEFUL SKY OF NEW BEGINNINGS

All our dreams can come true, if we have the courage to pursue them.
—Walt Disney

Baliawas is a small nondescript village. It is a cluster of small mud houses, nothing like the more glamourous Gurgaon, which has put the state of Haryana on the global map.

This is a true story. A story about conviction and courage: of not giving up against all odds, of hoping for a better future for their ill daughter. The parents in this story are illiterate and from a small village. Philanthropists helped them save their daughter.

India is a country of contrasts and great complexity. The picture is not simply one of rich versus the poor. The enormous challenges for development are the marked disparities amongst different geographical regions, between social groups, amongst different income levels and between the sexes, which make life a challenge even for couples like Aman and Anil, who think differently.

This quiet village is the home of a few hundred families. Anil and Aman are amongst those who live here with their three children. Anil's mother lives with the couple, whereas the father lives further down the same road with Anil's brother. They come together every day as a family and pitch in to get the work done to earn their living. Life is not easy for the family, who have seen better days.

The birth of a child brings with it hope for a better tomorrow, and the couple were optimistic. It was a bitterly cold winter in November 2012, when Anil and Aman celebrated the birth of their second child, a daughter, putting aside the misgivings of the extended family. The birth of a girl child even today is considered a scourge in many parts of India. Overcoming the muttering within the community, they decided to name their daughter Anjali, which means 'gift' or 'offering'.

It was almost prophetic; her life, the family was going to realize as she grew, was indeed a gift.

Anjali's elder brother was three years old and bored at being an only child. He was thrilled when he saw her for the first time, reaching out to touch her, disappointed that she could not chase him immediately nor join in his games. He felt cheated, having waited for her to be born and burst into tears.

'Shshsh...'. His mother consoled him as he was led away by Anil. 'She will grow up in no time', he was told, 'and then she will run faster than you and climb trees like a monkey'.

What neither he nor the family realized was that Anjali would not be able to play like a normal child and would not climb trees. Anjali was different. The doctor had been brutally frank. 'Your daughter has been born with a heart condition, a CHD'.

Seeing their bewildered look, the doctor had tried to tell them as best as he could. Big words were used, and both

Anil and Aman had been reduced to tears when they heard that their little baby had Tetralogy of Fallot. They did not understand what it meant but the serious look on the face of the medical team reduced Aman to tears. 'It cannot auger well', she told Anil.

There was a hole in the lower chamber of the heart (a VSD), and if this wasn't scary enough, there was also narrowing of the pulmonary valve, which is commonly known as pulmonary stenosis.

The family gathered to discuss their options. They turned to the health worker in the village, scrambling to look for answers. They rushed to the local doctor, the one the whole village consulted. Differences forgotten, the entire community rallied round them and helped them take the baby for her first consultation.

They walked out of the clinic armed with a long list of medicines that had been prescribed for her. Confused, they could only pray that she would be cured, and their nightmare would end soon.

Every morning, Anil and Aman woke up looking at the rising sun, hoping for a miracle. 'The new dawn brings so many possibilities, today will be the beginning, Anjali will get better', was their affirmation to each other. This was a daily chant; each one said it louder than the other, hoping that their God would hear as they dressed their son for school.

Anjali turned four as their third child was born. With the passage of time, their hopes were dashed; they could no longer fool themselves or explain her lack of energy.

She had reached a school-going age, where her days should have been filled with school and games. Instead, Anjali was at home; school was becoming a distant dream for the family as her physical decline was apparent. She was tired and continued to languish at home, whereas children her age raced past their home on the way to school. Aman would cringe when she heard them.

Their meagre earnings meant money for consulting a specialist was a strain. With three children and rising expenses, it was nearly impossible to make ends meet. Anil had given up farming and was a tractor driver because it paid more, and he needed a regular salary.

The local doctor who they had been consulting over the years referred them to a charitable foundation. Anil made the call. He prayed fervently that the nameless person at the other end would listen to his story and hoped that there would be help for his little Anjali. As he waited for the phone to connect, he kissed his talisman, 'miracles happen' he told himself. 'Miracles happen to people like us', he told himself trying to drown his despair.

The call was the miracle Aman and he had prayed for. The voice at the other end assured him of help, and promised that Anjali would be taken to a specialist and given the required medical intervention. Anil told them that he was not going to be able to contribute financially, that his meagre salary of ₹8,000 was not enough for his family of five.

The foundation, he was told, would step in to financially support the medical expenses if required.

Anil was ecstatic and rushed to tell Aman, stroking Anjali's head as she innocently clapped her hands because her parents were happy, not comprehending the cause for the excitement.

The family got up at dawn and said their prayers before making their way to Max Hospital, in Saket, New Delhi, a two-and-a-half-hour drive on a tractor muscling its way through Delhi. They were buoyant that their worries would soon be behind them and that their lovely little daughter would get the much-needed treatment.

On arrival, they were ushered into the clinic, so different from that of their local village doctor. They were in awe of the place and of the medical team that seemed to crowd the little consultation room. Anjali was examined; she was then quickly plugged into machines, which made Anil and Aman nervous.

Anjali, they were told, is critical, even a day's delay could have been fatal. While at the hospital, little Anjali began to give in. Brave until then, her body shuddered, and she collapsed. If they had arrived moments later, it might have been too late for her as she had to be resuscitated immediately.

The focus was on stabilizing her. Aman and Anil were devastated.

After hours, Anjali was stabilized, and the echo test showed that her pulmonary artery had not grown and was small for her age. She needed a BT shunt immediately. However, Aman and Anil declined the operation because they needed time to arrange money for it. Aman pulled together the meagre family savings, but the ₹25,000 they could find was never going to be enough.

No time could be lost, so the charitable foundation agreed to financially provide the remaining amount so that the surgery could take place.

Assured that Anjali would be operated upon, the couple was relieved, but their happiness was short-lived. Apparently, post-surgery, Anjali required focused medical care, and the chances of infection were high, Aman and Anil were told.

The doctors also explained that there would most probably be more than one surgical intervention. Aman broke down; her muffled sobs could be heard down the corridor while Anil stared ahead in stoic disbelief. It was a lot to take in.

Anil's mind was racing. He had many questions, 'How much more could his daughter endure?' 'How are we going to afford this?' 'What sort of life is this for such a young child?'

He controlled his fears and spoke reassuringly to Aman while the doctors operated on Anjali. That was the longest hour in his life. Finally, they were told the surgery was over. It had gone as planned, successful.

Aman and Anil clutched their lucky talisman and looked out at breaking dawn; the bright orange and pink in the morning sky was a sign of hope and of a new beginning.

They spent the 12 days needed for Anjali's recovery in the hospital, some hours seemed to stretch when anxiety got the better of them.

In late July 2017, she was finally discharged from the hospital and taken back to Baliawas.

Her grandparents and her family were overjoyed. Her brother danced, and her little sister ran behind their mother just to catch a glimpse of Anjali.

Aman and Anil had been told that they had to keep Anjali on a regime of long-term follow-up. The first check-up was due after a month, and it would continue up until the next surgery.

It was the middle of an Indian summer, long days and warm evenings. Anjali was oblivious of the sweltering heat and the electricity shortage. Her body was healing, and she lay still recovering on the small bed, often for what seemed like eternity to her watchful family. Even if a fly landed on her cheek, she lay still, fast asleep as her body struggled to heal.

When awake, she watched her little sister play while waiting for her elder brother to return from school. Anjali's recovery was slow; the wounds from the surgery took time to heal. There were moments when Anil and Aman despaired seeing Anjali's discomfort and slow recovery.

Anjali, as it happens, did join her brother in school, but it took time. It was in 2018 when Aman and Anil finally decided to enrol her in Krishna Vidya Jyoti School, the same school as her brother.

It has been a long and lonely journey for her. Prior to her first surgery, she could not even get up from the bed without assistance. She needed her parents or grandmother to walk her to the toilet, so school had seemed a distant, if not impossible, dream.

At first, Aman was a little reluctant—she feared for her daughter's well-being. She was unsure of Anjali fitting into a school routine after the surgery. What if she fainted or worse?

Aman and Anil finally made a big decision; they enrolled Anjali in school and decided that it was her education and not her marriage which was a priority. This raised eyebrows in the village, where the norm was to marry off a daughter as soon as she hit puberty.

Unlike most mothers in the village, Aman's ambition for Anjali was focused on her getting a future; she wanted her to study, get a job, earn for herself and live an independent life. And she along with Anil worked relentlessly to ensure this, breaking with tradition and refusing to give up on her daughter.

Anjali is now in nursery, and has adapted well to her surroundings. She has made some good friends, and teachers say that she is a fast learner and has a sense of humour!

In October 2018, Anjali was taken back to Max Hospital for her second surgery, which was successful. She is now back in Baliawas, waiting to rejoin school. She wants to study hard so that she can one day be a doctor and treat little children, like the Doctor Aunty who saved her!

15
THE CHANGE MAKERS

Above all be the heroine of your life,
not the victim.
—Nora Ephron

THE AARA PROJECT: PRIYAL AND ANAMI GULIANI

Delhi is the capital of India and is a bustling metropolis. This is the heartbreaking story of a couple who lived and worked in Delhi. The story is in the words of the mother; it is full of emotion and straight from the heart, a mother's heart.

'My husband and I are self-made; we are professionals and have worked for more than a decade in high-profile jobs. We thought we had seen it all. We have had the privilege of being educated in some of the world's premier institutions; we found jobs and have done well in the terms used to describe success conventionally'.

'We thought that our experiences and exposure helped shape us and that we were aware of the world around us and we assumed that we were where we belonged in the corporate world having earned our spurs'.

'We were wrong. Life is lived forward, but it all makes sense when we look back'.

'We were elated; I had just given birth to a little girl in 2016. My husband and I were thrilled, she had been welcomed by both our families; the joy was infectious until the moment the medical team at the high-tech hospital broke the news'.

'The shock left us numb. We were told that our little daughter had been born with a congenital defect and needed immediate treatment. This is our story'.

'This was our introduction to the world of paediatric cardiology. Before this, I didn't even know such a specialized field even existed!'

'It didn't sink in easily and didn't for a long time. Life, they say, is a punching match and often hits you with a boxing glove. I was constantly wondering, "Why me? Why us?" There are so many children born every day, why does our baby, our precious daughter need to suffer?'

'However, subsequently when I visited hospitals and clinics, and saw the queues of anxious parents clutching onto their children, I realized I was not alone. We were not singled out to suffer; that this was more common than I had realized'.

'With a handful of experts in the field across the country, we chose what we were told were the best in the field'.

'My personal journey opened the window to a world I knew little about—children born with CHD'.

'Being a reporter, I covered stories on the insurance sector. My first story, I remember, was on policies that involved children. In 2004, there was huge debate on these and similar issues, and as a result one of the exclusions in these policies was CHD. I still remember asking someone at that time, 'What does it mean?' And I found out years later when confronted by it. Life has a way of catching up.

'I remember one of the doctors telling me after examining my daughter—A hole in the heart is nothing! And my understanding until then was—A HOLE IN THE HEART! OH MY GOD! I was mistaken again. CHDs are of various kinds; to be honest, I have forgotten the count. A lot of them are curable, with surgical intervention. One needs constant monitoring, but the child can live an "almost" normal life'.

'I was told this repeatedly by the specialists we took our daughter to. Repeatedly by several doctors on many occasions'.

'But then there was a catch. Not many could afford the treatment'.

'In our journey we saw several children recovering, some even within a few days. And there were other cases that reduced us to tears. There was this one baby who had been in the hospital virtually since birth and by the time we left the hospital it was already seven months for him in the ICU'.

'We also saw many cases where the children did not survive and other cases where families had to take tough decisions because the medical treatment was unaffordable and beyond their reach'.

'Some have sold their houses, took loans, others approached NGOs. During these three months, I met a gentleman working for a charitable foundation. This foundation is for children suffering from CHDs. The gentleman I met was the head of paediatric cardiology at the foundation and was raising funds for the same. We met at the hospital as he had come for a child; the foundation was sponsoring this boy's treatment'.

'He described how he helped children and their families cope. Some of the stories were heart-wrenching. He shared with me how they lost one baby because the parents could not afford the surgery and when they found a hospital that had the team and facilities for the same, they were given a date three years later for the surgery!'

'I remember our first day at Jaypee Hospital in Noida where one of the finest doctors in the field performed a miracle almost every day'.

'We met a family from Mumbai whose 12-year-old son was getting discharged after being brought in an air ambulance to Delhi. Most hospitals in Mumbai had given up on him but not his parents. In them I saw a reflection of my husband and my determination. We were not going to give up on our daughter'.

'And here they were gleaming with joy after getting discharged soon and giving us much-needed assurance, strength and comfort. This was in the month of March'.

'Unfortunately, in May, when Aara, our daughter, was still in the ICU, we saw the same family come back'.

'The boy had developed an infection and had to be treated for six weeks. We met every day and became each other's support system, drawing strength from our shared concerns, mapping our children's progress.

'When Aara was moved in the room from ICU, they were in the ward next to us. The boy and I used to play scrabble in our precious little free time; for him it was a distraction from the pain he was going through and for me it was the much-needed hope that refuelled my determination and weary spirit'.

'A few days after we were discharged and brought Aara home, we got to know that the injections which were supposed to work like miracles for the boy were not helping, and he had to undergo another major operation'.

'The boy's family did not have money for the operation. His father called Anami, my husband, and told us his inability to raise funds. Anami then created an account for him in a crowd-funding website by the name of Milaap, and in three days after exceptional support from his office colleagues and some of my colleagues and friends, we managed to raise funds close to ₹400,000 and his surgery was successful'.

'Today he is back in Mumbai and we feel good to have been part of his journey'.

'However, the universe wasn't as kind to us. Our daughter Aara did not make it'.

'The day Aara left us, Aara's compassionate doctor told me that our daughter not only touched our lives but helped save the life of the 12-year-old boy'.

'After few months, I picked up the courage to go out and meet the team of the Genesis Foundation'.

'Our life's mission became clear. For as long as we live, we are determined to help children with heart issues'.

'Together with Genesis Foundation, we have started The Aara Project. It is dedicated to children suffering from CHD, who have limited, or no means to seek, medical assistance. The project aims to educate and create awareness about issues under paediatric cardiology and to help families and children'.

'Aara means "bringing light to lives" and this is what we intend to bring into these families by raising funds and supporting children'.

Priyal Guliani, Aara's mother, is a former editor, anchor and producer. She has worked in premier business new channels of global repute. Anami, Aara's father, is an in-house legal counsel of a leading global oilfield services company in the United States. Anami and Priyal have dedicated their lives to raising funds to support children suffering from CHD.

. ~.

PURKAL YOUTH DEVELOPMENT SOCIETY: G. K. SWAMY

At 82, G. K. Swamy is convinced that he has miles to go before he sleeps. His dreams are big because they include the hopes of 530 students studying at the school he founded in 1998.

Twenty-two years ago, he left his job as an Economist in Mumbai and a happy coincidence brought his wife, Chinni, and him to Purkal. They had rented a place in Dehra Dun, close to Purkal. They set up home and looked forward to a different life from the one they had in Mumbai. The corporate life had taken its toll on Swamy's health and no longer enticed him. He had seen it all: the big corporate salaries, the corner office and so on. Swamy was highly stressed in Mumbai and had become diabetic. He travelled 20 to 25 days in a month. His wife and he yearned for a simpler and quiet life.

Life had other plans, and his life would not be nearly as simple or quiet as he had wished it to be. Swamy noticed that underprivileged children in his rural community stood no chance in gaining employment next to their wealthier peers, and he decided to do something about it. He began an after-school tutoring programme to supplement the education of four local children at their home. Cattle sheds and garages were their gilded halls of learning. These children brought their friends, and the friends brought more. Soon, they shifted into the guest room and spilled into the verandah.

As the numbers grew, a strange thing happened. The house seemed to shrink but their hearts expanded. They hired a cow shed to accommodate the growing numbers. Often the parents were too poor to send their children to school or if the children were in government school, they came to Swamy to learn more and to cope with homework. Some came for the food they were served along with the class.

A chance remark about how he should start a school egged the Swamys to take a bold step. They identified the land, raised the money from friends and well-wishers and did exactly that. And so began the exciting PYDS.

Purkal is a sleepy little village in the foothills of the Himalayas, on the outskirts of Dehra Dun. In 1998, Dehra Dun had not been touched with the development seen today, growth which has yet to touch Purkal's 5,000 inhabitants, who remain largely dependent on activities such as farming. Usually, there is only one earning member in the family and most are caught in the desperate cycle of survival and struggle, not finding a way to be part of the development story around them. The situation was even worse a couple of decades ago.

'In those days, poverty and unemployment defined life in Purkal and the surrounding villages, especially after the factories were shut down', says a local villager, 93-year-old Satteshwar Dangwal, describing the Purkal of old. 'We lived on what little earnings cultivating our small pieces of land would bring. We tried to marry our girls off at younger ages, while alcoholism swallowed our men'.

Children did not have access to quality education, good role models and enough exposure. This is precisely what made Swamy step on. What was once a small organization to help children with their studies is now a full-time school, with the vision of overall well-being of the children. Established in 2008, with the help of numerous altruists and donors, the well-equipped school now has over 500 students. Yet the class size is restricted to 25 students per class. Interestingly, about 75 per cent are girls because the school believes that educating a girl changes a generation.

The Purkal school provides mentorship, healthcare, nutrition and an education of the highest order to children who would otherwise never have gotten it. Swamy's vision is unique because it does not end with academics; PYDS works with the children through school and beyond. They help them prepare for university, mentor them after university to get jobs. They feel each child deserves a future and must work to his best ability. They often help the children at their school to move to better schools, often raising the money for their fees or helping them get scholarships.

Enrolling children with potential from deeply needy and underprivileged families, preferably from the remoter reaches of Uttarakhand, PYDS provides these children with holistic care and education, including life skills and value systems through a combination of adequate nutrition, healthcare, high-quality academics and full exposure to the co-curricular. It strives for excellence, and its philosophy is to run a contribution-driven, caring and giving ecosystem that enhances each and every life it touches.

An alumnus of this school, Ankit Nautyal, was awarded the Brightest Young Hire Award at KPMG recently. Ankit is an engineer and, prior to KPMG, he was with Infosys. His mother was the cook at the school when Ankit enrolled at the Purkal school. Today, she is employed with the school and is very proud of her work as the cook.

Mayank Sharma graduated with top honours from the Purkal school but has returned to work at the school. He wants to give back to the school for he firmly believes that it opened out a world full of opportunities for him. He knows the difference it made to his life and to that of his friends.

PYDS also tries to empower the rural community by helping them by educating them, providing health services, establishing skill development projects giving employment and preserving the beautiful Himalayan environment, local cultural traditions and the sense of community. It encourages women empowerment, working with local women and youth since 2000. PYDS helps them through income generation, various community development programmes and additionally provides career counselling to the children from their early stage.

Swamy humbly says, 'I don't know whether we thought of this as our life's work or our mission. We did think that we'd invest our best into the few children we had in the early stages. The few became many, not at my instance, but because many people thought that it was a good input that the few were getting'.

. ~.

EVERY STEP MATTERS: RADHIKA BHARAT RAM

> *Learn to light a candle in the darkest moments of someone's life. Be the light that helps others see; it is what gives life its deepest significance.*
> —Roy T. Bennett, The Light in the Heart

'I believe empathy is important in whatever work we do. Whether it is education or social work, one needs to be empathetic in both the cases because only then can lasting and sustained impact be created', were Radhika's opening words to me. She belongs to a world of privilege and prestige but feels a deep responsibility to give back to society. Her biggest concern is that her two children should understand and recognize the same; that it is their duty to give back to the universe especially when they come from a position of privilege. There is joy in making a difference to someone else's life.

'And what is not known widely', said Radhika, 'is that in giving there is a getting back too, but not in the form most would recognize it. There is unadulterated joy, pure and sublime, especially if there is no agenda attached to the giving. Most often the people helped by us are not known to us'.

Her mother-in-law, Manju Bharat Ram, spent less time at the institutions that she was best known for, The Shri Ram Schools in Delhi NCR, as compared to her time at The Blind School. Radhika calls her mother-in-law her Guru, and it is that example that stoked the desire in Radhika to do something for the cause that she contributed so much to. While Radhika jointly chairs the School board, working with the Blind Relief Association is something that she holds dear.

However, what she is driven by is in the fight for early detection of cervical cancer. Cervical cancer is the second most common cancer amongst women and is the primary cause of cancer-related death in developing countries. In India, cervical cancer is the most common form of cancer, and the awareness is so low that it is disturbing. Radhika decided, with a small team, to embrace the cause, working tirelessly to educate and inform people at the local village level and even in Tihar jail. She also joined the three-year-old CAPED—Cancer Awareness, Prevention and Early Detection that has been working in the area of awareness creation for women centric cancers—and took its journey forward. There has been a regular campaign against cervical cancer for 30 years in India, but this has had little impact on the morbidity and mortality from the disease, with India ranking fourth worldwide. According to January 2019 data from the National Institute of Cancer Prevention and Research, India, over 96,300 new cervical cancer cases are detected in the country in a year, with over 60,000 deaths. The cancer mostly affects women (between 40 and 55 years), especially those from the lower economic status who fail to carry out regular health check-ups due to financial inadequacy.

'Most women even after detection shy away from treatment. In the villages, we talk to the Panchayat and are often dismissed as 'women's problems'. No one takes it seriously and then it is too late'.

Every year, cervical cancer is diagnosed in about 500,000 women globally and is responsible for more than 280,000 deaths. There is a wide variation in the incidence of cervical cancer across the globe. In the west, early detection through regular screening has aided to significantly control the prevalence of this disease, thereby lowering its incidence. In the last 50 years in the United States, Pap smear tests have reduced the deaths related to cervical cancer by three-quarters. Cervical cancer was once one of the most dreaded cancers and the leading cause of death.

Today, there is a vaccine to prevent cervical cancer. However, awareness regarding its importance needs to be communicated. People even in the so-called affluent segments of society are not always aware that it is essential for their girls. The need to focus on the preventive vaccination is a priority. Girls in schools must be vaccinated, and since men are the carriers, boys need to be aware of and take the vaccination as much as girls. Human papillomavirus vaccines (HPV vaccine) is commonly used but is not licensed everywhere for use amongst males. Efficacy studies amongst males are under way. Australia is the first country to approve the quadrivalent HPV vaccine in males (between 9 and 15 years old), and the vaccine was approved for administration to males between the ages of 9 and 26 years in other developed nations. It is a fallacy that this is a women's problem alone. It is much larger than that; it is a concern for humanity. Two vaccines licensed globally are available in India; a quadrivalent vaccine (Gardasil marketed by Merck) and a bivalent vaccine (Cervarix marketed by GlaxoSmithKline).

Starting from her desk, Radhika has reached out to thousands through her work with cervical cancer patients as well as generating much-needed awareness about this illness. Let's talk about it; let's talk cervical cancer and let's do something about it. These slogans drive her and her team of volunteers. 'Some *bastis* and slums have a higher incidence of cervical cancer; we track areas and then place them on a priority'.

Juggling her various commitments, driven by the desire to do something, Radhika carries on. If each one helped one person of their choice, spent some time listening to another human being, the angst in the world would be reduced and the happiness quotient will significantly rise.

. ~ .

TRANSCRIBE: MADHAV LAVAKARE

Madhav Lavakare stood silently at the school citation ceremony as the principal of his school read out a long list of accomplishments. Madhav is a teenager and looks like one. Looks are beguiling and his big smile hides a big heart. For, at the young age of 17, he has received the Pradhan Mantri Rashtriya Bal Puruskar 2019, along with other awards.

Altruism and philanthropy come in different forms, and millennials do things in deeply impactful ways. They have the ability, for instance, to focus on a problem that needs fixing and then take direct action. While generations older than them tend to use institutional structures for impact, millennials present effective, well-thought-out and direct-impact solutions. An example is the 16-year-old Greta Thunberg from Sweden, whose activism for climate change sparked protests/demonstrations across Europe.

Madhav Lavakare, similarly, is a doer, and his solutions used technology. 'Here's where I come into the picture', he said. 'I've always been a kid with a knack for finding the wackiest solutions to all sorts of problems. To me, problems aren't problems—they're just solutions waiting to be found. And I love finding them'.

'Over the years, as I've worked with technology to find solutions to problems, my evolution as a problem solver has brought me an important realization. The powerful idea that technology is just a tool to solve big human problems in the world, and that technology, no matter how attractive or mind blowing, can never be anything without that human aspect attached with it. A community, like the hearing-impaired that has been neglected, can use technology as a choice to mainstream itself—not just helping its individuals, but also contributing to the greater good—that's the power of technology when you use it for good'.

'I've often seen initiatives for other minority groups and disabilities', said Madhav. 'There are a plethora of apps and tech devices, for example, for the visually impaired or those with learning disabilities. But rarely have I seen initiatives aimed at having a deep impact on the hearing-impaired community. They are truly at the bottom of the pile, the most under-represented and marginalized community. People with hearing impairment often find it infinitely difficult to integrate into mainstream society. Sometimes, that may not be what they want, but at least they should have that option. Like everyone else, this community has enormous potential skills and contributions to offer to the world. Unfortunately, and especially in India, it is very rare to find the hearing-impaired living a life of dignity and independence and earning a respectable livelihood'.

His deep interest in technology led him to fall in love with Google Glass—and he was crushed when the device failed in the market. Around the same time, Madhav had experienced how someone with hearing impairment finds it extremely difficult to interact with the world around him. One of his friends who was hearing-impaired left his school because he couldn't manage being in an environment surrounded by hearing-enabled people.

So Madhav set about building a wearable assistive device that could caption conversations and speech on a heads-up display in the user's field of vision, eventually developing Transcribe—a device that aims to solve the problem of the communication gap that exists between the hearing-impaired and the hearing-enabled.

Along the way, Madhav feels he's learnt many more skills than he ever did in school. What he's also learnt is the meaning of nuance.

'I've learnt that the deaf aren't just the "deaf"—a homogeneous community, even though some of them treat that as their identity and are proud of it—but that there are layers and nuances that one can only understand by interacting with them at a deeper level, immersing myself in that community, I've learnt how to say "I've made an assistive device to convert speech to text" in sign language. And I love to see their faces light up when they try on my device', says Madhav.

'But most importantly, I've learnt that you don't look at the hearing-impaired community as a burden on society—you see them as lost potential of a community that could contribute to the world in such a big way. They're not a community that needs outsiders help them by giving them handouts—they're a community that has been neglected and sidelined but has the potential to do something big if they are provided with the tools to help themselves. What I'm doing is not, and never was, social service. It's not about parachuting into a neglected community for some time to help them, and then when I'm done, that's the end of that. Rather it's about unlocking the untapped potential of an entire people, some who may be more talented and accomplished than some of us sitting in this room, so that they have the option of integrating into mainstream society if they want. I am not helping them, I am helping them help themselves'.

'Why am I doing this? Because I want people who are different from us to find their own dignity and to contribute to and feel proud of contributing to the greater good'.

REFLECTIONS

Why is a person born with everything in life, while another must struggle to eke out a living? A silver spoon for some and not even crumbs for another? It is often said that before an individual act, there is freedom but the implication of the actions will follow whether we want it or not. An arrow once shot cannot be recalled.

And the same is true for our state of mind.

'I used to think that I can turn the world around as I wanted. I could do anything I wanted to do, when I wanted to. And then life happened. I was expecting my second child when my insides prolapsed and I was bedridden. I could not move because my baby was in stress'.

'Losing a child has given me happiness. Strange as it sounds, the loss made me different, not better, not worse but different', Prema said, balancing her coffee in her hands as she looked out of the glass door.

'I gave birth after a long surgical intervention to a premature child. The baby turned blue/purple within minutes and was no more within 24 hours. I was numbed; nothing made sense. I saw my doctor crying and told her that I had had a premonition when I left home that I would be coming home alone. My voice was flat and completely devoid of emotion'.

'The trauma remained bottled within me during the day but at night I could not sleep. 'Why Me?' The question was like a coiled snake; it poisoned my nights and plagued me by day'.

'When my friend Pankaj Baliga called to say "Hi, haven't heard from you for a while". I told him about the loss of our child. Soon after I received a book from Pankaj, *When Bad Things Happen to Good People* by Harold S. Kushner. I started reading it. This was the turning point in my life'.

'My doctor told me to divert my mind—go to Mother Teresa's home and one afternoon when the noise in my head was at an all-time high, I drove to Old Delhi'.

Kushner's words came to me:

'Seek something outside your nine-to-five job as an additional source of fulfilment and as a way to feel the joy of helping others' (Kushner 1981).

'It changed my life. I saw newborn children with no parents, rows of cribs with tiny children being looked after by the sisters who were clearly stretched and grateful for an additional pair of hands'.

'I held a bottle with one hand while an infant drank milk, sucking greedily and with the other patted another baby to sleep. I noticed how the few volunteers were mostly foreigners and then saw a shape lying alone at the far end of the long hall. A bed facing the wall, alone and isolated'.

'When the baby was done feeding and the other had fallen asleep, I walked across the room. I cannot describe what I saw, I don't have the words. I saw a child who was living but dead. He stared at the wall mutely; his eyes were open, but soulless'.

'A few questions and a little prodding helped me understand his situation', Prema said with kindness and empathy reflecting in her eyes.

. ~.

Growing up as a military kid in the cantonments of a small town in India, Prema was a wild child whose 'Swiss blood ran one way and the Indian blood another way'. She was born to a mother from Switzerland and a father in the Indian Air Force, from Sindh, now in Pakistan. Raised in a home with a services background, discipline, fighting all odds, and seeking uncharted territory was in her DNA. However, from riding a bike to breaking ranks from her father when she wanted to set up her own printing press with her brother, Prema never backed down from a challenge. Speaking of her childhood, Prema says, 'Every answer to my question to my dad was a No!'

This early opposition made her a risk-taker at work with a strong drive to find her own way. At the same time, her values from her disciplined Air Force father kept Prema grounded. In service class families, it is never about not what you get, it is about what you do. 'The more my dad said no to me, the more I did things'.

Discipline was not the only value Prema learnt at home. Helping others and giving was also something she grew up seeing and imbibing. One of her fondest memories with her mother is going with her to the Blind Relief Association every Sunday. At the school run by the association, there would only be one book in Braille in every class. Her mother learnt how to write in Braille and started spending long hours creating books for the children. She even tried to raise money to import Swiss watches with Braille markings, but, unfortunately, she could not. This selfless giving inspired Prema and sowed the seed of helping others in her—a seed that has grown into a flourishing tree over the years. The legacy of giving continues in her family as her daughter Simran joins in her philanthropic endeavours.

A college dropout, Prema never believed in doing the conventional. From a receptionist's job at a law firm to starting a printing press and then a magazine called *The City Guide*, she strayed far from the norm and took the path less trodden. 'My mother always said I was born that way. She felt that I would do what I wanted to do even from the time I was born'.

Prema quit her parental home, at age 22, with one suitcase in hand to get married. When you have run away, you are free. Sagar's personal life was full of the unconventional too. She ran away to marry a then budding lawyer of the time from the firm where she worked as a receptionist. Now known as one of the finest lawyers in India, Jyoti Sagar continues to be Prema's biggest support.

'My husband, Jyoti, never said No to me for anything'. So, when Prema wanted to set up a printing press, she did so in partnership with her brother. Success did not come easy. Her first project as a printer—clients included hotels like Maurya Sheraton—had a tough start. She and her brother were new at the business and did not know how to cost things well, ending up under-budgeting and taking losses from time to time. It did open more doors for her, though. And she carried on and brought out a city guide next, before eventually moving to 'public relations'.

Running the press and then starting the city magazine, Prema learnt that no task was too small and none too big.

These were the first seeds of entrepreneurship that she sowed, and at a time when there were not the vast resources that entrepreneurs have access to today.

In the course of running the printing press, Prema came in contact with Priya Paul of The Park Hotels. At that time, The Park Hotels was looking to promote itself but not by spending a tonne of money on advertising. Priya's father had been unfortunately assassinated by suspected militants and the hotel had barely any occupancy. With no understanding nor idea of public relations, Prema helped the hotel organize a series of events called 'Going Public at The Park', a monthly talk event over tea and cookies. The event gave visitors a sample of what The Park had to offer and that led to a rapid rise in the occupancy rate. From there, she added two other clients, interestingly all in the travel and tourism business.

With this, Prema took her first steps in public relations and realized she wanted to get into it more seriously. In November 1992, she set up Genesis Public Relations. It was the right time for a firm like this because the Indian economy had just opened its doors for foreign companies to invest. While, on the one hand, these companies came in expecting someone to manage public relations for them, they also awakened Indian organizations to the need for public relations. In this way, Prema did not just set up her own organization from a basement office, she also led the charge in laying the foundation of what is today a thriving, vibrant industry.

In 2005, Genesis was acquired by Burson-Marsteller, a part of the WPP group. This made Genesis one of the first home-grown public relations firms to be bought over by a global communications giant. Prema Sagar continues as chief executive of the business, now named 'Genesis BCW' (part of Burson, Cohn & Wolfe). She is also the founder president of the Public Relations Consultants Association of India, an organization that encourages sharing of best practices in the industry along with being the founding member of the Public Affairs Forum of India, which was created to bring similar levels of collaboration and knowledge sharing in the public affairs realm.

'Someone just has to say, Prema, you cannot do this. And my goodness, I just have to do it!'

Inspired by Mother Teresa, Prema established Genesis Foundation, a trust created to provide access to world-class medical care for abandoned and underprivileged children facing life-threatening ailments. Her courage and determination led her to start this foundation—the genesis of which is her second-born son she lost to a congenital heart disorder 34 years ago.

'I don't really think it; it's really from the heart'.

The foundation, of which both Prema and her husband are trustees, is now focused on facilitating critical life-changing and live-saving treatment of children from underprivileged backgrounds suffering from congenital heart defects.

Jyoti Sagar, her husband, has been the pillar in Prema's life. Besides being her anchor, he is an eminent lawyer, an expert in corporate and intellectual property law.

After having spent early years of his professional life in a law firm, he started a solo practice from a one-room office in Delhi. The practice—J. Sagar Associates—he founded is now one of the leading corporate law firms in India. He co-founded another firm—K&S Partners, which is an Intellectual Property Law boutique and is a leading national practice in that space.

'When I started in the profession', says Jyoti, 'lawyers basically did what came their way. In the early days of my career, I could be handling a matrimonial dispute in the morning and a technology transfer agreement in the afternoon. That was a time everybody did everything because the opportunities were limited. That has very significantly changed over the last two decades. The distinction is not only between contentious practice and non-contentious practice, but even within those broad practice areas there are very acute specializations'.

But what makes Prema and Jyoti's eyes light up is their Genesis Foundation.

'We believe that every child has the right to live a healthy life, and that is why we started Genesis Foundation—an organization which has, since then, evolved'.

'We had a vision—where we wanted to make a difference to the lives of little ones who suffer from life-threatening ailments, and who have every right to live life, healthy and happy. They can't be denied that right because of lack of funds. Genesis Foundation has seen this vision come true… as we aspire to Give Life a Chance'.

Over the years, this journey has become about more than Prema and Jyoti's passion. It has built a community of volunteers and supporters, each with their own motivation to work at the foundation. Their own inspiring stories of victories.

Or people like Priyal Guliani, a respected journalist, and Niren Chaudhary, CEO, Panera Bread, whose personal tragedies motivated them to join forces with the Genesis Foundation. Priyal lost her baby Aara to congenital heart disease and channelled her loss into supporting the treatment of other such kids, starting The Aara Project, aligned with the Genesis Foundation. Niren and Aditi's daughter Aisha lived a short but inspirational life, motivating others even as she battled inevitable death. Niren and Aditi too turned their loss into a mission to help others, putting his weight behind the Genesis Foundation.

The passion in the Genesis Foundation team is infectious and has led to large organizations lend their support to the foundation. While their fundraising events draw sponsors from across industries, the WPP CSR Foundation became the first global group to choose Genesis Foundation as its CSR implementation partner. While their vision was to support education and skill development, they aligned their support with Genesis Foundation realizing that before education, before skills, before anything, there is life. And, therefore, Giving Life a Chance is the first critical step. Today, the WPP CSR Foundation is supporting Genesis Foundation by funding the treatment of close to 100 children every year.

And, then, there are those silent givers, donating at every chance they can get, but not wanting to talk about it.

These stories, just a few amongst many, create a ripple effect, sparking more stories, more missions and, ultimately, more lives saved.

BIBLIOGRAPHY

Aknin, L., C. P. Barrington-Leigh, E. W. Dunn, J. F. Helliwell, J. Burns, R. Biswas-Diener, I. Kemeza, P. Nyende, C. E. Ashton-James and M. I. Norton. 2013. 'Prosocial Spending and Well-being: Cross-cultural Evidence for a Psychological Universal'. *Journal of Personality and Social Psychology*, 104: 635–652.

Al-Khalili, J. and J. McFadden. 2014. *Life on the Edge: The Coming of Age of Quantum Biology*. London: Bantam Press.

Andreoni, J. 1990. 'Impure Altruism and Donations to Public Goods: A Theory of Warm-Glow Giving'. *The Economic Journal*, 100(401): 464–477.

Andreoni, J. 1995. 'Warm-glow versus Cold-prickle: The Effects of Positive and Negative Framing on Cooperation in Experiments'. *The Quarterly Journal of Economics*, 110: 1–21.

Anik, L. B. 2009. *Feeling Good about Giving: The Benefits (and Costs) of Self-Interested Charitable Behavior*. Boston: Harvard Business School.

Aspinwall, L. G. 2003. *A Psychology of Human Strengths: Fundamental Questions and Future Directions for a Positive Psychology*. Washington, DC: American Psychological Association.

de Tocqueville, Alexis. 1835. *Democracy in America*. London: Saunders and Otley.

Danner, D. D. 2001. 'Positive Emotions in Early Life and Longevity: Findings from the Nun Study'. *Journal of Personality and Social Psychology*, 80: 804–813.

Darwin, C. 1859. *The Origin of Species by Means of Natural Selection*. London: John Murray.

Dawkins, R. 1976. *The Selfish Gene*. Oxford: Oxford University Press.

Duckworth, Angela and James J. Gross. 2014. 'Self-Control and Grit: Related but Separable Determinants of Success'. *Current Directions in Psychological Science*, 23: 319–325.

Dunn, E. W. 2008. 'Spending Money on Others Promotes Happiness'. *Science*, 319(5870): 1687–1688.

Dunn, E. W., Lara B. Aknin and Michael I. Norton. 2014. 'Prosocial Spending and Happiness: Using Money to Benefit Others Pays Off'. *Current Directions in Psychological Science*, 23(1): 41–47.

Evren, Ö. and Stefania Minardi. 2017. 'Warm-glow Giving and Freedom to Be Selfish'. *The Economic Journal*, 127(603): 1381–1409.

Fredrickson, B. L. 1998. 'What Good Are Positive Emotions?' *Review of General Psychology*, 2(3): 300–319.

Fredrickson, B. L. 2001. 'The Role of Positive Emotions in Positive Psychology: The Broaden-and-build Theory of Positive Emotions'. *American Psychologist*, 56: 218–226.

Fredrickson, B. L. 2002. 'Positive Emotions Trigger Upward Spirals toward Emotional Well-being'. *Psychological Science*, 13: 172–175.

Fredrickson, B. L. 2003. 'What Good Are Positive Emotions in Crises?' *Journal of Personality and Social Psychology*, 84: 365–376.

Gneezy, U. and Aldo Rustichini. 2000. 'Pay Enough or Don't Pay at All'. *The Quarterly Journal of Economics*, 115(3): 791–810.

Goleman, D. 1995. *Emotional Intelligence: Why Can It Matter More Than IQ*. New York: Bantam Books.

Han, S. L. 2007. 'Feelings and Consumer Decision Making: The Appraisal-Tendency Framework'. *Journal of Consumer Psychology*, 17: 158–168.

Harari, Y. N. 2015. *Sapiens: A Brief History of Humanking*. London: Vintage Books.

Harbaugh, W. T., U. Mayr and D. R. Burghart. 2007. 'Neural Responses to Taxation and Voluntary Giving Reveals Motives for Charitable Donations'. *Science*, 316(5831): 1622–1625.

Harford, T. 2006. *The Undercover Economist*. London: Hachette.

Isen, A. M. 1987. 'Positive Affect, Cognitive Processes and Social Behavior'. *Advances in Experimental Social Psychology*, 20: 203–253.

Jasper, C. R. and A. K. Samek. 2014. 'Increasing Charitable Giving in the Developed World'. *Oxford Review of Economic Policy*, 30(4): 680–696.

Kahneman, D. 2015. *Thinking, Fast and Slow*. New York: Farrar, Straus and Giroux.

Kahneman, D. and A. Tversky. 1982. 'The Psychology of Preferences'. *Scientific American*, 246(1): 160–173.

Kushner, Harold S. 1981. *When Bad Things Happen to Good People*. New York: Random House.

Lewis, M. 2016. *The Undoing Project: A Friendship That Changed the World*. New York: W. W. Norton & Company.

Malthus, T. R. 1798. *An Essay on the Principle of Population,* Chapter II. London: Oxford World's Classics.

Marshall, F. 2013. *Louden Nelson: From Slavery to Philanthropy*. New York: Marshall Publishing.

Mayer, J. D., P. Salovey and D. R. Caruso. 2008. 'Emotional Intelligence: New Ability of Eclectic Traits?' *American Psychologist,* 63(6): 503–517.

Murty, S. 2017. *Three Thousand Stitches: Ordinary People, Extraordinary Lives*. New Delhi: Penguin Random House India.

Okri, Ben. 2017. *Grenfell Tower: A Poem*. London: Financial Times.

Olson, M. 1965. *The Logic of Collective Action: Public Goods and the Theory of Groups (Vol. CXXIV)*. Boston, MA: Harvard University Press.

Prince, R. A. and K. M. File. 1994. *The Seven Faces of Philanthropy*. San Francisco, CA: Jossey-Bass.

Sheldon, K. M. 2004. 'Achieving Sustainable New Happiness: Prospects, Practices, and Prescriptions'. In *Positive Psychology in Practice,* edited by P. A. Linley, 127–145. Hoboken, NJ: John Wiley & Sons.

Sidibe, Gabourey. 2017. *This Is Just My Face: Try Not to Stare*. Boston, MA: Houghton Mifflin Harcourt.

Singer, P. 2009. *The Life You Can Save: Acting Now to End World Poverty*. New York: Random House.

Sundar, P. 2013. *Business and Community: The Story of Corporate Social Responsibility in India*. New Delhi: SAGE Publications.

Sundar, P. 2017. *Giving with a Thousand Hands: The Changing Face of Indian Philanthropy*. New Delhi: Oxford University Press.

Williams, G. C. 1966. *Adaptation and Natural Selection: A Critique of Some Current Evolutionary Thought*. Princeton, NJ: Princeton University Press.

ABOUT THE AUTHORS

RATNA VIRA

After a successful career where she worked at the CXO level in multinational and leading Indian corporates, Ratna Vira turned to writing fiction in English, with her work highlighting issues of deep social concerns. Her first book, *Daughter by Court Order*, was a national bestseller, reaching fourth in the Indian fiction lists in 2014, and it was featured in *The New York Times*. In the book, she talks boldly about issues of feudalism, patriarchy, and the rights of women. This theme was carried forward into her second book, *It's Not About You*, which was in the list of 35 Top Fiction and Non-Fiction Books of 2016. The book is about a single mother dealing with the school and the world when her son is found battered, beaten and bullied at school. Ratna is presently working on her third fiction book, which again holds up a mirror to the society.

Ratna's creativity extends to art. She is amongst the few Indian authors who write and paint. She is known for her charcoal paintings and mainly makes faces that express the different facets and stories of life and the world. The eyes in her charcoal paintings speak of the stories within, the struggles and the experiences of the people she draws.

She did her Masters from the London School of Economics and Political Science, UK, and is an alumnus of St Stephen's College, Delhi. Ratna has been a guest speaker at leading schools and universities, including Oxford and Cambridge, international business schools and has spoken at literature festivals and has also been part of several distinguished panels.

SUHASINI VIRA

Suhasini is a second-year undergraduate student studying Economics and Politics at Durham University. She has been awarded the Laidlaw Scholarship for Research and Leadership. For her scholarship research project, she is analysing the priorities and effectiveness of youth employment policy in India. She is the Co-Chief Editor of the *Durham University Economics Journal* and the Editor, Business and Economics, of the university's online magazine, *The Bubble*. She spends her free time sketching, dancing and bingeing shows on Netflix.

It's great to see a book capturing the magical journey of Indian football being written. I wish *India's Football Dream* and its authors Mr Shantanu Gupta and Mr Nikhil Sharma the very best, and hope it serves as a tool to educate every Indian about the 'beautiful game' in our country.

Praful Patel
President, All India Football Federation

A book about how Football has grown as one of the most loved sports in India.

For special offers on this and other books from SAGE, write to marketing@sagepub.in

Explore our range at
www.sagepub.in

Paperback
978-93-532-8305-6

> *Lynch Files* is bound to make a sensitive reader feel the meaning of being born as Akhlaq or Mohsin Shaikh in a non-secular/non-spiritual culture that allows the nasty politics of 'gau rakshaks' to insult the foundations of a civilization nurtured by the likes of Kabir and Tagore. A must-read!
>
> **Avijit Pathak**
> Professor of Sociology,
> Jawaharlal Nehru University, New Delhi

Shuddering accounts of mob lynching across India in recent years.

For special offers on this and other books from SAGE, write to marketing@sagepub.in

Explore our range at www.sagepub.in

Paperback
978-93-532-8219-6

Ilaiah Shepherd's evocative memoirs reveal the struggle for education and dignity that a great majority of Indians undergo. As a little boy herding sheep and goats, he and his brother were the first in their family to go to school. The author writes of his long and often interrupted journey to becoming a writer and an intellectual, without support and having to overcome adversities. In English, this is the first written account of growing up in an OBC family and covers social issues that affect those regarded as the lower castes.

A chronicle of the author's childhood and his eventual rise as public intellectual.

For special offers on this and other books from SAGE, write to marketing@sagepub.in

Explore our range at www.sagepub.in

Paperback
978-93-8134-541-2

Extolled for his extraordinary courage, Bhagat Singh is one of our most venerated freedom fighters. He is valourised for his martyrdom, and rightly so, but in the ensuing enthusiasm, most of us forget his contributions as an intellectual and a thinker. In the current political climate, when it has become routine to appropriate Bhagat Singh as a nationalist icon, not much is known about his nationalist vision. This book provides a corrective to this by bringing together a majority of Bhagat Singh's writings, some of which were hitherto unavailable in English.

A collection that brings together Bhagat Singh's seminal writings.

For special offers on this and other books from SAGE, write to marketing@sagepub.in

Explore our range at
www.sagepub.in

Paperback
978-93-528-0837-3